Advance praise fo

"A significant work in the fie   idies, *Ethics and the Craft* cuts straight to the heart of the matter. Covering everything from the Wiccan Rede to the Threefold Law and everything in between, Coughlin forces readers to question and explore both the foundation of Wiccan ethics and one's own relationship to them. This excellent dissertation is highly recommended to any Craft practitioner seeking to understand the little discussed--and frequently misunderstood--realm of ethics in modern Witchcraft."

Raven Digitalis, author
Shadow Magick Compendium & Goth Craft

"At a time when the Wiccan Rede is plastered all over the internet, and Karma is referenced in books that have nothing to do with Eastern religions, John J. Coughlin has offered up an invaluable guide to ethical considerations in the practice of Wicca. Along with dissecting such common near-platitudes such as the Threefold Law, he delves into highly controversial territory, to include blood in magic, the conundrum of money in exchange for spiritual practices, and even the ethics of publishing poor-quality books on neopaganism. Instead of imparting dogma, he offers up plenty of food for thought. This book is wonderful not only for facilitating independent decision-making regarding ethics, but is an effective item for smacking people who insist on repeating the same tired old arguments that they've given no real thought to. "

Lupa, author and editor for Immanion Press
Webmistress of PaganBookReviews.com

"I found myself in awe. This work by John Coughlin is so very much needed in our day and age. *Ethics in the Craft* not only clears up the history on both the Rede and The Three Fold Law, but also covers modern issues, such as Etiquette and money. The author goes into a great deal of depth in how we process ethical decision making, and applications of ethics in general. I highly recommend this educational and eye opening book."

Corvis Nocturnum, author
Embracing the Darkness: Understanding Dark Subcultures &
Allure of the Vampire: Our Sexual Attraction to the Undead

"An incisive and insightful literary endeavour into the world of Wiccan ethics. John Coughlin has both artfully and academically examined the ethics of the Wiccan religion and the outcome will prove useful to many, if not all, Wiccans today. A commendable and ethical treatise on a broad and obscured topic."

Gede Parma, author
Spirited: Taking Paganism Beyond the Circle

"John Coughlin has written a book that desperately needed to be written; a historical, critical, and incredibly well-thought-out analysis of Wiccan ethics. *Ethics and the Craft* is comprehensive, mature, useful, and vital to our development as a religion and a tribe. It belongs in every coven and solitary's library."

Dagonet Dewr, author
Sacred Paths for Modern Men
Past President of the Pagan Pride Project

Ethics and the Craft

The History, Evolution, and Practice of Wiccan Ethics

Other books by John J. Coughlin:

Out of the Shadows: An Exploration of Dark Paganism and Magick

Liber Yog-Sothoth

Cthulhian Grimoire of Dream Work

Visit JohnCoughlin.com for more information about the author.

Ethics and the Craft

The History, Evolution, and Practice of Wiccan Ethics

By John J. Coughlin

 Waning Moon Publications

NEW YORK, U.S.A.

2009

Revised second printed edition published by
Waning Moon Publications, LLC
Post Office Box 79
Cold Spring, NY 10516
USA
waningmoonpublications.com

Publisher's Cataloging-in-Publication Data

Coughlin, John J.
Ethics and the craft : the history, evolution, and practice of Wiccan ethics / by John J. Coughlin.
p. cm.
ISBN: 978-0-9823549-0-2
1. Wicca. 2. Religious ethics.   I. Title.
BF1566 C63 2009
299-dc22

                                        2009932474

ISBN-10: 0-9823549-0-8

Cover design and graphics rendering by Nicole Graf, nicolegraf.com

To Carmencita.

Hang in there!

Contents

Acknowledgements

How does one begin to acknowledge all the people who have contacted me over the last several years I have been working on this project and shared with me their experiences and encouragement? I am indebted to Margot Adler and Raymond Buckland for being kind enough to respond to the inquiries of an unknown researcher, filling in some blanks the books could not. A special shout out to Shea Thomas of the *Wiccan Rede Project*, whose own independent research into Wiccan ethics showed me I was not alone in having such a passion for this line of work. Special thanks to David R. Jones who opened the door for me into King Pausole at a time when I was hitting dead ends. There was a friendly soul at Villanovan University who took the time to look up an article in the school's newspaper from 1972 to help confirm a reference. There is Larry K. who... wait, he didn't really do anything – but he's ok. My wife Nicole of course, for helping me with all the little things I toss at her all the time and putting up with my fixations on my Work. I can't forget Raven Digitalis and his kindness in getting me in touch with some Pagan authors for endorsements and feedback, all the more important since my reclusive ways often limit my own networking.

There is just no way to account for *all* of you but know that this book is a reflection of all those who have at one point or another taken an active interest in this project.

Introduction

Ok, I admit it; I am one of those grumpy people who will quickly complain about the quality of many of the books on the Craft today and what impact that has on newcomers. It's easy to complain, but what good is that? Talk is cheap, and with the advent of personal blogging, rants are about as common as flies on a pile of dog poo on a hot summer day. Why not make a contribution toward a *solution* instead of sitting back and finding new and colorful ways to articulate my dissatisfaction, however over-critical it may be?

My complaint – so I can get it off my chest in one paragraph – is that there has been a tendency to package Wicca as "wicca-lite"; a watered down version of the "full version." This analogy works well to describe the growing trend, as Wicca has become more mainstream. Many software products offer a "lite" version that is either free or very cheap. The lite version has some of the basic bells and whistles for those who either don't want to make a commitment to the product or are just trying it out, but lacks the advanced features that serious prolonged use would require. Those who are serious about the product either go straight for the full version or upgrade from the lite version once they feel it works for them.

In the case of Wicca, the full version is hard to find among the hype and fluff, and instead of money, it requires a spiritual commitment. After all, Wicca is more than a system of magic – even more than a religion; Wicca is a *way of life*.

I shouldn't be so negative, of course. There are definitely good books and respectable authors out there and a whole new generation of authors full of promise and potential are entering the arena, ready to meet the challenges of today's world. It's just frustrating to see the good books lost in a sea of material that caters only to the public's fascination with the Craft.

With this mini-rant out of the way, I am now free to present the rest of this work in as non-biased a form possible. My goal is not to tell you how I feel Wicca ought to be, but rather to encourage critical thinking and foster a deeper understanding of Wicca as a true spiritual path. Wicca has changed over the years. Some of these changes are for the better and some of them are not. This is the price to be paid for a living religion that is not (theoretically) weighed down by doctrine or dogma.

I am concentrating on ethics because with all the aspects of Wicca that have been misunderstood, ethics has been one aspect that has moved to the forefront, sometimes being taken to the point of fundamentalism. Yet for all the attention, it seems that few really appreciate the depth and complexity of Wiccan ethics that transcends a few popular catch phases.

As I will no doubt state *ad nauseum*, this project is a continual work in progress and I welcome – if not encourage – you to share your own insights and research to help fill in the gaps. I make no claims to being an authority on the subject, although I have put much time and energy into my research over the years.

In researching the Rede and other aspects of Wiccan ethics, I was reminded of just how much has changed and how far we have come since the 1950s. From small, private circles hidden behind closed living room blinds, to huge public rituals in parks in the center of cities, it is humbling to be reminded of our simple roots. In a world that has become so small and interconnected with technology, and so much more accepting of our ways, it is exciting to consider how future generations will shape the Craft.

About this book

This book is essentially comprised of two parts. The first part is intended to be a general discourse on ethics, particularly from the perspective of the Craft, to help encourage critical thinking when dealing with ethical situations. While I am sure some of my own perspectives on ethics will be reflected in my writing, it is not my intention to favor any one ethical theory, but rather encourage the reader to develop his or her personal ethical stance.

The second part of this book is to share my exhaustive research on the history and evolution of Wiccan ethical ideas such as the Wiccan Rede and the Three-fold Law. This has been a labor of love for the last decade, and while much of my work can be found on the internet, this book takes that material to the next level, having been corrected and expanded from that original body of work. I would never say it is truly "complete" since there will always be new discoveries to be found, but do feel it has reached a point where it needs to be published in book form, both to educate and encourage further research.

I feel that this is the time to take such research seriously. We have already seen the passing of many first – and even second – generation modern witches, and with their passing many of these "little things" are lost forever. Such "little things" are our heritage, and as more time passes, the harder it will be to find and document them. Many of the books I researched that were published in the 1960s and 1970s are already out of print and often quite expensive to obtain (as I can attest!). If we don't strive to save this information now, what will future generations have to reflect upon?

I am by far not calling for fundamentalism or blind duplication of the older ways, but rather stating that in our constant striving to grow, we must never sacrifice our past. In order to understand Wiccan ethics today, one must know the context in which it was originally intended. Only then can we fairly determine how they may be adapted to fit the times.

You can help further my research!

I am always seeking old pagan/magical magazines, newsletters, and journals which reflect attitudes and beliefs at a given period of time, as well as indicate what influences were in play when the publications were first printed. Sadly, these are the very materials I find the hardest to locate, as they were more easily damaged or discarded than books over the years.

Please consider donating your used publications and old books (if you are not using them) so that I can further my research into the modern history of Wicca (and Paganism in general) and protect our heritage. I can only hunt down and purchase so many a year!

For my current contact information visit JohnCoughlin.com.

A Discourse on Ethics in the Craft[1]

Before we explore ethics in Witchcraft, we need to make sure we understand what we mean by ethics and morality. Generally, ethics are a set of shared values or moral principles that modify our behavior in social situations. Ethics attempt to set a standard form of conduct that we can all reasonably follow. The etymology of the words *ethics* and *morality* relate to "custom" or "manner" in both Greek and Latin. As popular Christian religions began to stress morality, these words took on a more religious connotation.

The complication in defining ethical behavior comes when we start to dig deeper. What are these "shared values?" How do we decide what is "right" and "wrong" when there are so many ways in which to view a problem? The more specific we try to be, the more likely we are to come across disagreements. It would be difficult, for example, to find exception to placing value on such qualities as truthfulness and avoiding harm to others, but which is more important when these values are in conflict? For example,

---

[1] This discourse was originally a chapter on ethics in a larger tome intended to be a true textbook on Wicca and Witchcraft that I have been drafting off and on over the last several years. I don't know if or when I will finish it but I feel this topic is so important that I decided to release it as a stand alone work along with my research into the history and evolution of Wiccan ethics.

if faced with lying to protect someone's well being, which value should take priority? Chances are this will depend on the *context* of the situation, but even then there is always the possibility that our views will differ. There are a number of factors which may make up the context of a situation – too many, in fact, to be able to plan for them all.

What is needed then is not just a set of shared values, but a framework on which to judge the weight of these values in the context of the current situation. We'll explore some ideas on how to do that, but first we need to see where Wicca stands when it comes to morality.

Ethics and Witchcraft

Since there are many forms of Witchcraft, we must be careful not to assume they all hold the same ethical model or share the same values. The truth is that for the most part, Witchcraft does *not* have a built in ethical system but rather relies on the personal sense of ethics of the individual. Some witches have no problems using curses to seek justice or get what they need, but usually a witch would consider the ramification of those actions before taking such drastic measures. This is especially true of the non-religious forms of witchcraft[1]. As we move into the more religious forms of witchcraft such as Wicca, ethics begin to be addressed within the belief system itself, but even this has changed greatly over the decades. While we will explore many of the ethical concepts of Wicca in this chapter it is important to understand that not all forms of Witchcraft and Paganism adhere to or accept these Wiccan concepts. Wiccan beliefs have been very influential in many forms and traditions of Witchcraft however,

---

[1] As in, witchcraft purely as a form of folk magic and not tied to any particular religion. Wicca, on the other hand, is a form of *religious* witchcraft which also happens to use folk magic, but the magic is not its primary focus.

so it helps to have a general understanding of the nature of those beliefs.

Ethics was not always a key subject of discussion in Wicca. Before the end of the 1960s, very little emphasis was placed on ethics at all. Being non-dogmatic, Wicca had no set ethical laws, and it was generally felt that ethics was best left *outside* of religion so as to avoid bias to any given belief system (ie, how can ethics be "shared values" if they favor one religion's views over another?) .

However, as Wicca began to grow exponentially, ethics began to take a forefront in emphasis. This was partly because many felt the need to defend Witchcraft from its negative stereotypes. It was also a reaction to the sudden increase in practitioners of the Craft who lacked the formal structure of a coven to keep them in check. Traditionalists believed that the coven was a grounding support that helped to keep members from reacting too hastily in an emotionally-charged situation, and thus the growing trend in solitary practice was an issue of much concern to them.

The reliance on ourselves to determine our ethics instead of some external authority is not an easy path, and to take such an approach one must be able to accept that mistakes are bound to happen and that we can either learn from them or live forever in doubt of our abilities.

Although Wiccans and Witches will vary in their ethical beliefs, there are a few common themes shared by the majority:

- Wicca and other forms of *religious* Witchcraft are spiritual paths that respect life in all its forms and so strive to cause no harm when possible. This is a common ethical theme in Neo-Pagan spirituality.

- Witches of any form accept that all actions, including the choice to *not* act, have consequences that cannot always be foreseen. Even the best intentions can cause unexpected suffering. We therefore try to remain aware of the likely consequences of our actions but accept responsibility for our mistakes or those times when things don't go as expected.

- Witches accept that, as humans, we are fallible. We will always make mistakes but we also know that we can learn from them.

The Wiccan Rede

Wiccan ethics center on the Wiccan Rede[1]: *If it harms none, do what you will.*[2] Longer versions have been created to add poetry, personal views, or both, but this one sentence is the basis of these variants and closest to the nature of Wiccan belief.

Origins of the Rede

When you hear about the history of the Rede you will usually be told that Lady Gwen Thomson introduced it to the Craft in 1975 through an article in the Ostara issue of *Green Egg* magazine that year.

But did you know Doreen Valiente mentioned the Rede in a speech in 1964? Valiente's quote was also published in early Wiccan newsletters such as *Pentagram* and *The Waxing Moon* between 1964 and 1966, but the Craft was still new and circulation of these early newsletters was low compared to what followed the explosion of interest that occurred in the United States in the 1970s, so Lady Gwen's version was published at the right time and the right place to spread quickly. Lady Gwen had a different poem or creed attached to the long version but both her version and that of Doreen Valiente end with the now famous phrase, *"Eight words the Wiccan Rede fulfill, An' it harm none, do what ye will."*

The Wiccan Rede is an ethical ideal of personal social responsibility. It is intentionally vague because Wicca is an open religion based on personal experience and practice. The Rede is a foundation to work on, not a framework to work in. In fact, the meaning of the word *rede* should keep its intention in the proper

---

[1] At least by nature of "harm none." Not all Wiccans may refer to the Rede itself.
[2] Sometimes instead of "if" the Old English "an" is used.

context; "rede" is a word from Middle English that means "to advise" or "give counsel" and does not mean law or commandment. Given the fact that Wicca is non-dogmatic, the foundation of Wiccan ethics as a suggestion keeps to the nature of the religion's flexibility and sense of personal responsibility.

On the surface, the Rede seems quite easy; especially easier than organized religions such as Christianity that demand adherence to a strict set of laws. However, as one begins to live by the Rede, it does not take long to discover how difficult it can be. What is harm? The more we explore it, the more complex it becomes. We constantly make decisions that directly or indirectly not only affect us, but countless others around us. These choices not only include our actions, but also our choice to *not* act. Sometimes, the greatest harm is caused by not acting when we could have.

The Rede forces us to think not only about our actions but the motives behind those actions and their consequences. Good intentions are not enough justification for our actions. Countless atrocities have been performed under the guise of good intentions, and often the perpetrators were sincere in their desire to "do good." The Inquisition, Nazi Germany, the death camps of Pol Pot – these are extreme examples of the same principle we see every day; fundamentalist Christians *mean well* in their attempts to persuade government to work according to their own sense of ethics, despite the fact that they condemn anyone who does not share their views. Terrorists see their attacks on the innocent as being for the greater good of their cause and are willing to die for their beliefs. New Age "fluffy" Wiccan extremists mean well when they ignore or condemn aspects of the Craft that could be misinterpreted as evil or dangerous by non-Wiccans and newcomers in hopes of getting on the good side of those who condemn Paganism, yet they can go to such extremes that they sacrifice the balance of their religion and deny its roots.

Additionally, the consequences of our actions may not always be easily recognized. For example, one could argue whether casual drug use is harmful when done responsibly and with non-addictive substances, but what one may not consider as readily is the source of those drugs. For example when such substances are being obtained from a stranger on a street corner, legalities aside, one may very well be funding prostitution, gang violence, and other harmful activities which one would not consciously condone. Ignorance does not lessen the impact of our choices.

To be responsible for our actions we must first understand the nature of those actions, and to do that we must understand ourselves. Of course we can't sit around contemplating a decision forever either. By living the Rede, we can find a balance of thought with action. This does not mean we won't make mistakes. Mistakes are inevitable. As Wiccans we must accept responsibility for our actions and learn from them. Through this process we will develop our understanding of ourselves, and how we relate to our environment. This is the heart of the Wiccan Rede.

Harming "none" also includes oneself, but how does one harm oneself apart from the obvious case of suicide? Self-destructive behavior is a common example, but often we are not aware of such behavior, as it usually has unconscious motivation. Addiction comes in many forms. Some, like drug abuse, are obvious, while others, like eating or shopping when we are depressed or lonely, are not so obvious. When do these seemingly harmless habits become abusive behavior? To be able to answer these questions we first need to understand the source of such behavior and how such behavior may be holding us back. The Rede thus encourages us to strive to better understand ourselves by exploring the aspects of ourselves that lie hidden to our consciousness.

A similar concept to the Wiccan Rede that has been embraced by many occultists, including some Witches, is a phrase coined by Aleister Crowley: *Do what thou wilt*. There are many who believe that this was an influencing factor in the development of the

Rede. Here the notion of *Will* must be defined since it does not infer a license to do anything one wants. By *Will*, one is referring to the true nature of one's being, and to act in accordance with that true nature. One of the goals of a magician is to discover one's true Will and learn to separate it from whims and social conditioning. Given much of our actions are based on "auto pilot" with little conscious consideration, this awareness is all the more challenging. Thus the significance of the popular magical maxim: *Know Thyself.*

Limitations of the Rede

The Wiccan Rede is not a complete ethical system, and this is important to understand because it is the most often overlooked aspect of Wiccan ethics. The Rede provides a foundation based on Wicca's core principle of the sacredness of life – yours, other humans, and all life. It provides a reminder as we make decisions to allow us to live as responsible Wiccans. It offers a starting point for your own inner dialogue about how to conduct your life. But that is where it ends. The Rede does not provide specific practical rules or a detailed structure to work with – that is left to the individual to discover.

In essence Wicca has no ethical *system*, just a reminder of the life-affirming nature of the religion itself. To be Wiccan is to respect life, and to respect life is to not intentionally harm it needlessly.[1] We therefore must seek our own ethical stance based on those principles, and there are many ethical systems with which to work.

I strongly recommend that you read several books on the philosophy of ethics so as to better understand the nature of the various ethical approaches. Some approaches are better able to work upon the foundation of the Rede than others, but any viable ethical system can be used. The specific ethical system you

---

[1] The Lycian tradition presents an interesting version of the Rede to address this: *An it harm none, do as you will. An it cause harm, do as you must.*

choose will help you better answer more complicated questions such as how to deal with competition where one must weigh one's own needs against those of others, or how to approach such controversial moral issues as polygamy or polyamory, drug use, euthanasia, or abortion, which don't necessarily have one ethical answer.

For example, in making an ethical decision, there are many ways to consider the consequences of your options; each ethical theory takes a different, but viable, approach to the decision.

- Which of the alternatives will result in the greatest benefit – or the least amount of harm – for the greatest number of people?

- Does the expected "good" your action brings about outweigh the possible harm that might be done to anyone?

- Will anyone who could be considered "defenseless" be harmed?

- Which of the alternatives is most based on your own best interest?

While the questions above consider the consequences, other approaches consider the nature of the choice or action itself:

- Are you responding to a perceived need or does your choice demonstrate a genuine concern for others affected by your decision?

- Is your decision something you would be willing to make a rule or policy that you and others would follow in similar situations in the future?

- Are you sure the intent of your decision is free from vested interest or ulterior motives?

Remember that "harm" is a very subjective concept and therefore it is essential that you develop a consistent ethical structure upon the foundation of the Rede. Inconsistencies leave room for abuse through one's biases, be they conscious or unconscious. No matter what system of ethics you decide to work with, as a Wiccan you must be willing to live by it responsibly and own up to your mistakes.

Remember also that your interpretation of the Rede is not the only one possible. Holding your views over those of another denies that person the freedom (and responsibility) to make his or her own decisions based on personal experience and insight. For example, you may find abortion to be harm to an unborn child, while another may find that denying an abortion causes harm to the mother's Will and needs. Such issues are complex and powerful in their arguments on both sides. The Rede does not offer the answer, but one's personal choice should have its foundation in the Rede. Wicca, as a religion, does not hold an official stance on such issues, for that is left to the individual to decide through debate and contemplation. Unlike an organized religion, Wicca demands that we all find our *own* answers responsibly. This takes both the courage to think for oneself and the wisdom to know when we were wrong.

The Three-Fold Law

The Three-fold Law, or Law of Return as it is also called, is perhaps one of the more controversial of Wiccan ethical statements, and is not embraced by all. Its basic premise is that anything we do comes back to us in the end, often to a greater degree (particularly three-fold although the Dianic Tradition holds a *ten-fold* return when harm is done to the innocent). If we do good, then good will be returned, and if we cause harm, we put ourselves in danger of harm. Ethically this is equivalent to the golden rule: "Do unto others as you would have done to you" or perhaps the common saying: "What goes around comes around." But in the case of the Law of Return, there is a literal reward or punishment tied to one's actions, particularly when it comes to working Magic.

The debate over the validity of the Law of Return and its variations takes many forms. Some feel that it was created to keep new initiates in check as they learned to work with Magic, while others feel it is a remnant of Christian thinking, being that a majority of Wiccans were raised as Christians. However, many Wiccans today, including some authors and elders, take the Three-fold Law quite literally.

Since the idea that "we reap what we sow" is generally accepted among Wiccans, the Law of Return as a theory of cause-and-effect can fairly be considered a core belief. However, it must be acknowledged that it is neither a necessary nor defining belief of the Craft, despite its current popularity. There are many Wiccans – experienced and new alike – who view the Law of Return as an over-elaboration on the Wiccan Rede, which recommends that we refrain from causing harm. The most common argument against the Law of Return as an aspect of Wiccan ethics is that a Wiccan would not wish to cause harm since he or she *deems it wrong* to do so, not out of fear of retribution.

So far we have looked at the Law of Return as a form of cause-and-effect which is linked to all actions. There is however another perspective that looks at the Law of Return as a principle specific to Magic. This perspective has been coined the *Boomerang Effect* and must be considered separately from the perspective of cause-and-effect as discussed above, because its context is much different. The general principle is that when directing energy towards a person, that energy will rebound back to the sender *if* it misses the target or is met with a stronger defense. In such cases the released energy will follow the path of least resistance, which would be back to its source. Stewart Farrar was a proponent of this theory, which was heavily influenced by the work of Dion Fortune and other early modern occultists.

This notion of the Boomerang Effect has also been used in conjunction with the general law of cause-and-effect, producing the belief that *any* energy that is sent out will eventually rebound back to the sender, even if it does hit its mark. This causes much confusion because all three notions of the Law of Return are quite common in Wicca and are often easily confused. When discussing this principle it thus is very important to understand the context in which it is being used.

In contemplating the Law of Return, one must also accept that life is not always fair; that bad things happen to good people and the "bad guys" sometimes get away with their crimes. However our actions are not based on fear of retribution or hope of reward; we live our lives with respect for ourselves and others and a reverence for life. After all, the focus of ethical decision-making is not on what we can get away with, but in doing the "right thing." Behavior cannot be considered ethical if we are being forced into that behavior, no matter how "right" it may be. Doing good because of one's convictions and doing good because one does not want to be penalized are very different in nature!

While the interpretation of the Law of Return varies among Wiccans, as a whole we accept that when we intentionally cause harm, we have likely planted the seeds of our own destruction. These seeds may never come to fruition, but since we don't live in a vacuum, anything we do for good or bane is *likely* to return to us in some manner eventually. We may choose to perceive this as a law of nature or simply a matter of common sense. For example, if I treat everyone I encounter with disrespect, I should not be surprised to find that when faced with a personal crisis, I will not have as many neighbors rushing to my aid as I would have had I earned their respect.

Why *Three*-Fold?

It was via the Gardnerian and Alexandrian traditions that the idea of a law of return was commonly expressed. In these traditions, three is a very significant number in ritual, particularly during initiation.

- There are three degrees of initiation in these traditions.

- The traditional Gardnerian magic circle consists of three circles: an inner circle surrounded by two outer circles.

- The circle is often circumambulated three times during ritual.

- When the magus rings the bell in ritual it is done three times.

- In second degree, the initiated returns the number of strokes of the scourge three-fold onto the initiator.

Additionally, in the Gardnerian and Alexandrian second-degree initiation ritual, the magus states, "Thou hast obeyed the Law. But mark well, when thou receivest good, so equally art bound to return good threefold."

It is easy to see that a three-fold law could easily be inferred by an initiate, particularly during the second-degree initiation. If one would receive good three times then it's easy to assume the inverse, and so bad deeds would result in a three-fold penalty. Whether this was actually intended to be taken literally or not is a topic of debate. Either way, many *have* taken it literally and taught it as such.

Karma and Ethics

Many Wiccans believe in some form of reincarnation, although it is not always clearly defined. With this belief in reincarnation is often the belief in Karma, where our actions ultimately determine the context of our next life. This belief in Karma is Hindu in origin, but began to interest modern Western thought in the late 19th Century with the rise of spiritualism and theosophy. In migrating Eastern thought to the West, however, some of the beliefs were misinterpreted due to cultural differences. For example, Karma literally means "action" in Sanskrit, and refers to the natural law of cause and effect. Anything we do or think produces both visible and invisible consequences. The invisible consequences are called our *destiny*. In the East destiny is seen as being fluid and based on our current environment and what influences have lead us to that moment. Since we are free to make our own choices, we can change our destiny. This idea is often confused in the West where we tend to view destiny as something blind and static. Additionally, modern Western culture is heavily influenced by Christianity, and so Karma is perceived as a system of reward and punishment based on our actions, reflecting the notion of Christian judgment. This is very different from the Hindu concept and is reflected in Wiccan thought.

It is not uncommon to hear Karma brought up when discussing Wiccan ethics. The three-fold law is considered by some Wiccans to be the manifestation of Karma in the present life. "Bad Karma" is often portrayed as having retributive properties, inferred by such expressions as "karmic backlash." Fear of Karma has manipulated many Wiccans into doing the right thing for the wrong reason, and thus would technically not make it an *ethical* principle.

While reading a book on yoga[1], I came across an interesting reference to Karma from the perspective of Hinduism and yoga. As expected, it discussed good and bad Karma and the process of "working out Karma," which is commonly heard in Wicca today. However, the book continued by stating that ultimately one did not want to create *any* Karma; be it good or bad.

This struck my interest for two reasons. First, in modern Western interpretations of Karma, it would be more common to hear that we must just create "good Karma" or somehow transform bad Karma into good. This yoga book however, taking Karma in context of Hinduism, stated the goal was to be free of all Karma. The second reason why this interested me had to do with the sudden realization that this was very much akin to Taoism, to which I have long related. In Taoism, one seeks to maintain

---

[1] George Feuerstein & Larry Payne, *Yoga for Dummies*, 1999, page 16.

"action without action." In other words, one learns to live according to one's own nature[1] and so any action we do is a natural response and not a product of conditioning, social pressure, guilt, etc. This is very much akin to seeking freedom from Karma in the Hindu perspective.

Getting back to Hinduism, any Karma, good or bad, is an attachment and Hinduism seeks to be free of all attachments. One must therefore go beyond good Karma to ultimately be able to break out of one's unenlightened state of consciousness.

Enlightenment to the Hindu is the permanent realization of one's true Self that transcends individuality (which Hinduism considers an illusion). Although the Hindu context of enlightenment is very different from a Taoist since the Hindu sees life as an illusion while the Taoist is more of a pragmatist, both seek enlightenment through discovering and following one's own true nature. This is also, interestingly, very similar to the goals of the modern magus, who seeks to discover and follow one's true Will and in doing so one essentially transcends ethics, since one's true Will would then be in accords with the Universe.

In discussing Karma as it is seen by many modern Wiccans, one has to wonder if the concept of Karma has been taken so far out of context in the West that it has lost its intention. When I see so much emphasis on Karma in Wicca, to the point of treating good Karma as a commodity to store away or earn like currency, I am inclined to think so.

Evil and Paganism

Wiccan ethics is not a clearly defined topic and operates under the assumption that the *individual* is responsible for both making a decision and accepting the consequences of that decision. This

---

[1] Which is believed to be intrinsically good.

is a far cry from what most of us have been raised to think. Western culture is heavily influenced by the Judeo-Christian concept of absolute good and absolute evil, being given an external set of laws (such as the Ten Commandments) that we must follow. We are also expected to follow the decisions of religious authority who interpret these laws for us. For example, although homosexuality and birth control are not listed in the Ten Commandments, the Roman Catholic Church was kind enough to decide on these issues for their flock and decreed them sinful acts. Unfortunately, the Church also wields considerable political power and openly strives to ensure that the world – Christian or not – also adhere to their standards.

In Christianity, the concept of evil is externalized as "the Devil," an entity who tempts us to sin while God is the manifestation of pure good. Sinful thoughts and emotions are also externalized to some extent until we cave into temptation. For example, some might argue that homosexuals were not naturally homosexual but that they allowed temptation to get the better of them and the seeds of homosexuality were thus allowed to germinate.

Pagans, on the other hand, do not base their concept of deity on moral principles. As a nature-based spirituality we see deity as transcending morality. The gods are neither good nor evil, just as fire or a tornado is neither good nor evil. Nature simply exists and life is bound in a cycle of life and death, complete with both the beauty and terror that is inherent the process. There is no moral judgment to the killing of life to sustain life. Life feeds on life and that struggle can be harsh. The preying mantis, for example, eats its victim alive; although disturbing to us, it is not "evil" but the harsh reality of the struggle for life from which we have become distanced.

To Pagans, evil becomes relative to human experience. Only humans (at least that we are currently aware) have the ability to transcend our instincts and animalistic nature. We can define our own path like no other animal. In doing so we can act in ways that are not in accordance with our true nature or Will. This is when evil comes into the picture. Evil is not seen as an external force, but an internal imbalance. Murder for petty reasons, deliberately causing unnecessary suffering, squandering our resources – these are manifestations of evil to Pagans. Evil is a human concept that can only be applied to humans.

Money and the Craft

Some Witches believe very strongly that money should never exchange hands in the Craft and a Witch must never charge a fee for classes or services. The logic is that when money is involved, emphasis is taken off the practice and onto profit. Money can have a sneaky way of creeping into one's thought process and when it begins to be the priority, the practice suffers. Some who keep to this school of thought prefer to keep the Craft small and communal so that the community remains a tightly-knit and supportive structure where ideas are shared freely and openly.

Although this would be ideal for many, it is not easy in practice. Interest in the Craft has already grown incrementally over the years and very few of us are self-sufficient enough to dedicate that amount of time and energy to teaching and servicing the community for free. It would be unfair to expect even the most sincere teachers to have to pay for all related expenses.

Those who believe a small fee or donation is acceptable believe the small fees can help weed out the idle curious from the sincere. With the increasing interest in witchcraft, free classes would be overrun with the curious, leaving less room and attention for those who are serious about their studies. It also eases the financial burden on those who have chosen to dedicate some of their time toward helping others. The fees help pay for supplies such as candles and incense and for space rental and maintenance.

I have seen many grove and coven leaders invest a considerable amount of money into ritual supplies without ever questioning or complaining, even when they have been unemployed at the time. But to expect them to take on the financial burden alone can be just as unethical as those that use the guise of community leaders or teachers seeking only to profit from those who don't know any better.

There is a huge difference between charging a small fee to help pay expenses and providing a service specifically for profit. It is usually not difficult to recognize the warning signs. Sincere groups and individuals will not emphasize the fee and keep it as low as possible, and those who cannot pay but are sincerely seeking to learn would never be turned away. Some leaders clearly lay out the total expenses and simply ask that if anyone can help to please do so at their convenience. Those who charge high fees and emphasize the collection should raise red flags and one should proceed with caution. Obviously if a group is renting a bus for a trip there will be more of a concentration on funds since the bus company will want payment in advance or at the time of departure, and will not share the organizer's lack of emphasis on fees.

Where you choose to draw the line is a personal matter, but one that should be considered. In my *NYC Pagan Resource Guide*[1] on the Internet, I am constantly faced with the question of which events to list and which are not appropriate. My general policy is that anything that seems notably higher than average for the same service will require further justification of that fee. For example, when most open circles are charging $5 a meetings and I see an entry for a $50 fee for a similar event, I have to question that. Granted, stores will be expecting to make a certain amount of profit to support the store and that is taken into consideration, but I draw the line when fees become extreme. I also stopped listing individual psychics since there was no way to separate the

---

[1] http://waningmoon.com/guide.

sincere from the charlatans. I am sure there are few reading this who condone the television psychic hotlines and spiritual advisors that clutter the airwaves with their fantastic claims and so-called testimonials. While there are some talented psychics with a sincere desire to help, they are rarely found on the other end of a "free" five-minute reading.

How much is too much?

Each situation must be considered on its own since there is always the possibility of special circumstances. For example, if a bus is being rented for transportation or if a paid permit is required to use a public facility, the fee will probably reflect that. Likewise, some well-known authors and other speakers charge a lecture fee (plus travel expenses), so that too would be reflected in the fee.

However, for typical one to two hour events or classes I tend to be wary and ask for justification if the fee is over $15. If it is over $25, unless special materials are included to explain the cost, I keep away. Remember that some events like to keep the number of attendees small to allow more personal attention, so the fee may be higher to compensate in order to meet expenses.

One sign to look for in determining the organizer's priorities is in their payment policy. If the fee is a suggested donation and/or options are available for those who can't afford it, then that is a promising sign. Remember too that there are unscrupulous individuals who take advantage of this flexibility to get out of paying even when they can afford it; this is not only unfair to the organizers but has been known to make organizers hesitant in offering flexible fee policies for those who truly deserver it!

Money, Fame, Glory, and Pagan Authors

It may seem ironic for a Pagan author to write about this, being that I am making a profit on the very words you are reading, but say it I must!

I am not in the least bit ashamed to say that I hope to make money in book sales. I have put much time, energy, research, and even money into the production of this book and I take great pride in the results. I also hope, of course, that this book will be meaningful to the readers and serve as a valuable resource to others.

The question to me is not whether it is wrong to write and sell a book about the Craft, or even necessarily a question of where one's priorities are. Did I write this book to make money or gain popularity, or did I write this book to make a positive difference to the Craft? All these questions are unfair in that one can write a very useful book only for money, and one can write a terrible book with only good intentions. Still, I cannot entirely rule out intention here.

What matters is this: Authors who are Pagan have a *moral obligation* to the Craft (if not the gods) to present true and accurate material about the Craft and to keep quality an unwavering priority. To cut corners for the sake of publishing a sequel or making a book more marketable is to sell out one's faith.

When I see books written after 1990 which still literally claim to be an (until now unknown) ancient traditional branch of the Craft, and yet consist of nothing but modern elaborations of the same old material mixed with personal opinion, I get worried. When I see books crammed with spells to meet a page quota and yet crop the sections on the deity and other core beliefs to a few paragraphs, I get sick to my stomach.

More and more books continue to pop up with less and less detail, yet crammed with pages of spells and pseudo-history. It is evident that many authors—whose names I withhold as a gesture of good faith—are writing to *publish books* and not to promote the foundations of the Craft. This may be acceptable to authors who have no obligation to the Craft, but for *Pagan authors*, this is an atrocity.

It was my own personal challenge to write this book to see if I (a relatively unknown in the Craft) could do any better. I may fail miserably in this attempt but my goal is simple: to provide as much detail and insight as possible while not becoming too dry or overloaded with facts. My focus and passion is not on marketing, fame, or profit, but on the material itself. No doubt I have just ostracized myself from the Pagan community, which has at times a tendency of lifting its authors onto pedestals which they may not have earned; but the fact remains, authors need to be held accountable for their books, and it is the Pagan community which holds the key (and responsibility) to quality control.

Although my own experiences in writing and promoting books have given me a new respect for authors, I also know for a fact that one cannot claim authority on a subject by the number of books which they have published. *Anyone* with a knack for writing and the time and patience to find a publisher[1] can be an author, especially when keeping to the basics. True talent and authority becomes evident in the *quality* of one's work. I realize publishers do not help in this matter, but they are in the business of selling books and thus are more likely to follow the interests of their consumers. If we return books which do more harm than good, and write to both publisher and author about our discontent, we may eventually see a change. If we respectfully question authors on their sources when they present information that seems questionable, they will remember to separate their opinions from true research and actually read the books they list in their bibliographies. Both opinions and academic research are welcome, provided the distinction is clear.

Magical Ethics

We have already discussed the general ethical stance of Wicca, which holds for both daily life and magical working. Above and beyond the Wiccan Rede and the various forms of the Law of

---

[1] With the advent of print-on-demand services anyone can publish a book with little or no money. This has allowed fresh ideas from those who might not interest traditional publishers to be given a voice, but has also released a flood of poorly researched and impractical garbage.

Return and Karma, there are a few other points of concern (and debate) among Witches that have to do with ethics and magic.

Asking Permission

The issue of requiring permission before working magic on someone's behalf is a topic of much debate in the Craft and requires further examination. From the point of view of etiquette, it is common courtesy to ask first before providing magical assistance since such an operation could be perceived as an intrusion of personal space.

Likewise, it is quite possible that the person does not want help for any number of personal reasons, or is not yet ready to be helped. For example, after the death of a loved one, some require more time than others to mourn, and attempts to "pull them out of depression" are both unwarranted and unwelcome. Such suffering is part of the healing process. Catharsis is rarely a pretty sight, yet when the smoke has cleared, we tend to be the better for it. There is also always the possibility that a Christian or other non-Witch may not want a witch working magic for them as it might compromise their own beliefs.

Of course, it is honorable to want to help, but such help should never be assumed to be welcome or forced upon others without good reason. This is also not to say there are no exceptions, and this will become more clear when we explore the process of making ethical decisions later in this discourse.

Since there are no cut-and-dry answers when it comes to asking permission, let's take a few examples and examine the various perspectives. I won't offer an answer but instead offer various alternative approaches to point out the hidden complexities. Try to consider all perspectives. Often, contradicting perspectives are *both* morally justified!

Example 1: Imagine if your closest friend was hit by a car and rushed into surgery. Is it then fair to work magic to help that person recover without first asking permission?

Some would argue that the accident may have been a part of some "master plan" or the result of one's Karma and so interference with this natural process would be unwelcome. Of course, one would also have to question whether their help would also be part of such a process or "plan"! Perhaps your friend would rather die than face the results of the accident, such as paralysis or deformity. This alone opens up a whole new debate over the right to force an unwelcome life, as we see in cases of euthanasia. Another issue of concern is the intention itself; are you helping your friend for purely selfish reasons? For that matter, is the fact that your intentions are selfish even an issue of concern? As you can see, at first glance what seems like an obvious example of when helping without permission makes sense, it becomes much more complex when you begin to contemplate various perspectives.

Example 2: A close friend is addicted to drugs and you wish to intervene. Again, we have many of the same perspectives as in the previous example; perhaps this is a needed lesson in life which does not require outside interference. It is also quite common for addicts to not want help despite the fact that their life is going downhill fast. Do they truly not want help or is that just the addiction talking? Are we truly going against their Will, or is this self-destructive behavior arguably their true Will? Is it our place to even make such a decision for anyone other than ourselves?

Magical Ethics and Pseudo-Metaphysics

The main goal of this discourse is not so much to define what is right or wrong, or even to provide a specific ethical model with which to work. The objective is to stress the complexities of ethical thinking and to emphasize the need to base such ethical decisions on sound reasoning. What I often find, is that the reasons offered as justification for a given ethical stance are not based on true reasoning but rather on a form of *pseudo-metaphysics*. Pseudo-metaphysics is the assumption of truth based on what sounds as if it could be true. While such explanations may make sense, at least at first glance, relying on such logic skirts the true issues at hand. Such pseudo-metaphysical explanations don't offer valid arguments but rather provide a quick excuse from giving the issue any thought.

For example, occasionally one will hear a pseudo-metaphysical explanation as to why one should not work magic on someone very ill or in surgery, especially when they do not know about it. The argument is that since the person may be on the thin edge between life and death, any sudden "jolt" of energy could "shock" their system and throw that delicate balance out of whack, possibly killing them. This may seem to make sense, but let's not forget a few things: we are talking about healing "life energy" and the "energy" we work with in Magic tends to be subtle. We are not talking about electricity here! The word "energy" is but a poor metaphor for the natural forces into which we are tapping.

This is not to say it is necessarily justified to work magic in such a situation, but that this pseudo-metaphysical explanation is avoiding the moral issues one should be considering, which we discussed briefly in the previous pages. It is the easy way out – a poor excuse for not getting involved.

Another interesting pseudo-metaphysical excuse has to do with asking permission on the astral plane. In healing circles one will occasionally find a group leader who will stress the importance of having the permission of the recipient of the healing *but* when such permission has not been obtained, it is ok because we can just go on the astral plane and ask now! While astral communication is not without possibility, it is not the most reliable means of communication and requires much practice.

Simply telling someone to close their eyes and "ask" the person in question while the group waits for an answer is unrealistic. First of all, not everyone practices astral projection, and to assume one can do this "on the fly" is presumptuous. Secondly, even the experienced will find difficulty reaching such a state under pressure. Again, we find a reliance on a convenient "escape clause" which has no basis in practicality other than to allow us to feel justified in taking action without permission from the recipient. In practice, astral permission is more likely cheating or kidding oneself; "let's pretend we are not compromising our ethics." Visualizing that we are asking our friend does not mean we are truly in astral communication with that person. Asking a *mental image* of the recipient if it is ok to work Magic for them and "hearing" that image accept does not mean the person has actually agreed. Wishful thinking, assumption, and peer pressure all need to be considered when determining if this technique provides reasonable moral justification.

Such pseudo-metaphysical thinking can be found imbedded in many of our beliefs, such as in conjunction with the Law of Return. On a public newsgroup, someone once asked the question of whether children who were too young to know any better were still subject to the Law of Return. Many of the responses offered rather complex metaphysical explanations as to how energy is directed with intention, and delved into how the Law "knew" the difference, or how parental punishment compensated for the Law having to "kick in." What resulted was an anthropomorphism of the Law of Return into a very complex and sentient system, rather than an ethical discussion. In trying to work backwards, starting with opinion and customized theory in order fit that opinion, the pseudo-metaphysical explanations brought us no closer to an understanding and only confused the issues, thus opening the way to arguments and further complex pseudo-metaphysical mumbo jumbo to prove their points over the others. Honestly, I am not quite sure the discussion should even have included the Law of Return to begin with, as the question itself already assumed a literal stance towards that law, which is but one interpretation. Part of the basis for such a question lies in the current trend towards fundamentalism and over-emphasis of ethical summaries not intended to be the end-all for ethical discussion. The question was unintentionally biased towards such a fundamentalist approach.

To be fair, any metaphysical theory will lack a solid foundation in scientific fact, since we are attempting to describe the behavior and interactions of unseen and immeasurable forces. Until such theories are proven false they can often be useful tools in the right hands. The problem with *pseudo*-metaphysics is in how the theories were developed. Metaphysical explanations are derived from observation, experience, and intuition. These experiences shape the theory. Pseudo-metaphysics, on he other hand, are based on assumption, speculation, and hearsay with the intention to make a point or justify an opinion. For example, in the case of asking permission using astral projection as a substitute for asking in person, we started with a problem: *How can I do this healing without permission?* The theory of asking "astrally" was developed to *resolve* that problem, and was not the end result of true metaphysical thinking. Perhaps it *could* work even to those who never practiced astral projection, and perhaps it did work for someone at some time, but to assume it will work for *everyone* regardless of their background betrays it as a poor excuse rather than a viable or practical theory. Just because a theory sounds like it could work does not mean it has any basis in fact.

Perhaps some clarification is in order here. The issue of pseudo-metaphysics comes down to acceptable moral justification. For example, if your best friend were rushed to the emergency room and your reason for working healing magic despite not having permission was something to the effect of: *I care about my friend and know her children depend upon her. I am confident that she would want anything possible done to keep her family together*, then you have reasonable moral justification for your decision. If, however, you were attracted to someone who is depressed after recently getting out of a bad relationship and your reason for helping was something such as: *I hate to see her suffer and I really want to date her, but she needs to get over that relationship before she would even notice me,* well...I can only speak for myself, but from the perspective of moral justification for working magic without permission of the recipient, it would seem a bit weak.

Pseudo-metaphysics provide a false sense of moral justification. Such excuses *sound* like they *could* work and therefore are accepted as convenient truisms to justify one's preferred choice. This same twisted logic is what fuels such statements as: *The negative backlash of the Law of Return can be cancelled out with a good action of equal or greater character.* This would infer: *If I kill someone I can make it up by saving the life of someone else.* Obviously this logic is flawed!

Ask a child or someone who has not yet taken a physics class: *If I were to drop a 100-pound and a 10-pound weight from a building, which would hit the ground first?*

One could say it *sounds right* to claim that the 100-pound weight would hit the ground first, but in reality both would hit at the same time! If not for the air resistance even a feather and a hammer would hit the ground instantaneously. This was proven by astronauts on one of their visits to the moon, where air was not a part of the equation.

Just because something sounds true does not mean it is!

If you wish to make a decision that lacks moral justification, you are free to do so, and such a decision need not make it wrong. However, hiding such decisions behind a pseudo-metaphysical excuse robs us of our moral responsibility and fools us into false sense of morality.

Black vs White Magic

Discussing the concepts of black and white magic is problematic since there are many varying definitions, some of which have no basis in ethics. Additionally, many prefer to be "politically correct" and use the terms *positive* and *negative* to avoid potential racial associations although as we will discuss shortly, this too can lead to confusion.

Black magic has been defined as:

- Any form of magic done for purely personal gain or related to the physical plane, such as working a spell to obtain money, buy a house, get a job, or find love. (ie, any magic not done specifically to evolve oneself spiritually.)

- Any form of magic done with the intention of causing harm or go against the Will of another.

- Any form of magic, regardless of its intention, which makes use of demons or other non-angelic or non-deity beings to do one's bidding, such as elementals.

- Any magic used in a lessening or diminishing nature, be it to harm an enemy or break a bad habit. (This would be related to the waning moon.)

Although it is not uncommon for Wiccans to use the ethical-oriented definitions of black magic as anything done to cause harm and white magic as anything done for the sake of healing or helping, this distinction is by far not universal to all Wiccans.

When it comes to magic, however, ethical labels are ultimately meaningless. Magic is magic; there is no difference in the process, only a difference in the intention of the practitioner or in the end result. Since intention alone is a poor ethical qualifier, as we discussed earlier, it is best to avoid labels completely and consider each situation on its own.

Grey Magic?

Occasionally one will come across the term *gray magic*, which adds further complexity to the obsession many of us have with labeling things. While there is no one standard definition for this term, there is generally a sense of neutrality or balance inferred.

The concept of working with both white and black magic equally makes sense when using definitions that have no ethical connotation. For example, from the perspective of black magic being for personal gain, a "gray magician" is simply one who uses magic for practical applications, sometimes for their own benefit and sometimes for the benefit of others. This is generally referred to as "low magic," meaning earth-based magic (as apposed to "high magic," which has more spiritual intentions). Likewise, when black magic is defined as being of a lessening nature and white magic as being of an increasing nature, *any* practitioner of magic would fall into this category.

However, when used in an ethical context, this term can become a feeble attempt to escape ethical responsibility. If, for example, one considers black magic to be intentional harm, then doing it less or alternating with occasional white magic does not make one less immoral if that harm has no moral justification.

The labels *white* and *black* in respect to magical classification are considered "politically incorrect" to some for a number of reasons:

- As we have already observed, these ethical labels are too vague to be of much use in practical discussion. There are so many definitions associated with these labels within various occult traditions that their context is often confused.

- The ethical dualism of good (white/light) vs evil (black/dark) is derived from Judeo-Christian imagery and does not fit the context of how dark and light are used in modern Paganism, where they are complementary aspects of a whole and not contradicting and separate. Clinging to such imagery leads to imbalance when applied to the

Craft.[1]

- There are many who feel the black/white labels promote racial prejudice and stereotypes. This is not always conscious but its effects can manifest in unintentional stereotypical thinking.

Because of these problems with labels, more specific and descriptive terms are recommended when discussing magic, remembering that there are not many "shades" of magic, just various ways to approach and use it. For example, magic done with the implicit intention to harm could be referred to as "baneful magic" and magic done with the intention to heal could be "healing magic," and so on.

Remember that even generic descriptives like positive/negative or creative/destructive are problematic when used in a generic ethical context. Healing magic, for example, can be positive/creative when boosting the immune system or mending wounds, or it can be negative/destructive when killing cancer cells or fighting infections.

Blood and Sacrifice

Of all the subjects in this book, the topics of blood and sacrifice are most likely to illicit strong reactions and heated debates, being considered taboo to many modern Pagans. The reasons will vary, but the most common reasons given today would be:

1. Pagans wish to counteract the stigma of blood sacrifices placed upon them by society and so wish to avoid any practices that will feed that stereotype and further such misconceptions.

2. Pagan religions, being life-affirming and nature-based, would have no need for shedding blood or sacrificing

---

[1] I cover this in much detail in my book *Out of the Shadows: An Exploration of Dark Paganism and Magick.*

a life. Our deities do not require such acts and would probably abhor them.

3. Such practices go against the ethical stance of "harm none" and thus are not morally acceptable.

Interestingly, the reasons given against using sacrifice by early modern Wiccans, such as Gerald Gardner, had more to do with the instability and unreliability of the energy released through the shedding of blood, and that Wiccans did not have need for such a practice since they were well-versed in other more reliable forms of raising energy, such as dance. Shedding blood was essentially considered a quick way for the less scrupulous to raise energy.

When it comes to animal sacrifice, there is no room for elaboration in Wicca. Animal sacrifice is not an aspect of Wiccan practice or other forms of Neo-Paganism. Probably the only exception in modern Paganism can be found in some variations of Asatru, although the context is important to understand. Being a recreation of the ancient faith of the Northern Europeans and striving for historical accuracy in its practices, their beliefs will not as readily reflect modern social norms.

Asatru recognizes that although their ancient ancestors celebrated the *blot* by feasting on an animal consecrated to the gods and then slaughtered, our modern needs and lifestyle are simpler today, so an offering of mead or other alcoholic beverage is sufficient. Some also celebrate through a "sacred barbecue" of meat bought in a store or obtained through hunting. The word "blot" itself is related to the Norse (Germanic and Scandinavian) words for "blood" and "sacrifice." The ritual consists of three parts, the hallowing or consecrating of the offering, the sharing of the offering with those present, and the libation to the gods.

In some religions, such as Santeria, animal sacrifice is a normal and accepted practice. Although many people in urbanized cultures find this offensive or frightening, the form of sacrifice must be taken into context with the culture. In the cultures from which Vodun[1] and Santeria are derived, for example, animals are raised for food at many households and regularly killed during preparation of the meal. Taking the life of an animal is a common occurrence. Since religion is so interwoven with the culture, ritualizing the taking of a life is not so surprising. Often the animal is consumed afterwards. When it is not, the meal itself was sacrificed. Where food can often be scarce, such a sacrifice of a food source holds great significance.

This seems out of place in more urbanized societies where we are detached from the slaughter and preparation of animals for our meat. Many don't see themselves as eating cow, for example, but rather as eating a specific cut of "beef." In such a society, the ritualized killing of an animal seems foreign and frightening. In the few instances where it has been accepted it hides behind words such as "Kosher" or "Halal" where one can remain safely distanced from the details.

> The Hebrew word *Kasheir*, or *Kosher*, means "fit" or "proper." When applied to food, the term indicates that an item is fit for consumption according to Jewish law. Animals and fowl must be slaughtered by a specialist, called a *shochet*, and then soaked and salted in accordance with Jewish law.
>
> Likewise *Halal*, when used in relation to food or drink in any form, means that it is permitted and fit for consumption by Muslims. Animals and fowl must be slaughtered in accords with Islamic law.

It is difficult for most Neo-Pagans (many of whom live in urban areas) to accept animal sacrifice as a form of religious devotion since sacrifice is not accepted as part of their respective culture. Additionally, Pagans must contend with the common misconception that Pagans perform sacrifices to "The Devil." It should therefore not be surprising that the various forms of Neo-

---

[1] More commonly known as "Voodoo."

Paganism that developed within modern Western culture have not included the notion of animal sacrifice into their practices.

The use of blood on the other hand, becomes a bit more complicated. Because of blood's powerful association with both life and death, blood has long had an association with magic and its use can still be found today. In instances where blood is used in modern forms of Paganism, it is drawn directly from the practitioner rather than from a sacrificed animal. Only a drop is used, being obtained through a small pinprick in a finger. Women have also been known to use a drop of their menstrual blood.

In Witchcraft, when blood is used, it serves as a binding agent in spells. Magical tools can be consecrated with a drop of the practitioner's blood to bind the tools to the magician. Likewise, blood can link a spell to the recipient physically, while the practitioner uses visualization to complete the link. Although a lock of hair or a fingernail clipping can also be a powerful binding agent, they do not have the same metaphysical (or for that matter, archetypal) connection as blood. Occasionally, one may also find a recipe for incense that lists a drop of blood with this purpose in mind.

Apart from use as a binding agent, the use of blood, even one's own, is believed by many to infuse the working of magic with one's life energy. Blood is believed to contain our very essence. The psychological factors alone – the sense of archaic power, mystery, and devotion one experiences in drawing and using one's own blood – can also be useful in charging the magic work.

A form of modern blood sacrifice that may be deemed appropriate for Pagans is through blood donations. Such an activity serves not only as an act of devotion, but as an act of compassion by helping to save lives.[1]

When it comes to using blood, however, it is important to remember that there are many Wiccans and other Pagans who are uncomfortable with the idea. In fact, while some will use a drop of blood in consecrating their new ritual tools, others take the complete opposite approach and strongly believe that a tool must be destroyed if it comes in contact with blood and that the ritual knife must never shed blood. This is an excellent example of how ethics in Wicca can easily conflict; while some find no concerns with using a small amount of one's blood for magical use, others find it a perversion of the Craft. Such radically different viewpoints within the same religion is why it is so difficult to define a core set of Wiccan beliefs, and why so many of the examples in this discourse offer various approaches while avoiding the favoring of one over the other. There simply is no one definitive Wiccan way, only a multitude of approaches.

Ecology and Ethics

As a nature-based religion, a discourse on ethics would be incomplete without including ecology. It would be hard to conceive of a Pagan carelessly tossing a wrapper on the ground or needlessly wasting natural resources. Yet every day it happens, and on reflection we may find that we ourselves are guilty of such disrespect of our environment from time to time.

---

[1] An interesting side note on ethics, religion, and the donation vs selling of blood or transplant organs: some religions, such as Islam, forbid the selling of blood/organs but make exceptions for their donation in cases where it saves the life of the patient. In the case of Islam, the premise is that while the practice of putting parts of one person into another is technically forbidden by Islamic law, Islam is a religion of compassion and thus allows for such exceptions (albeit this interpretation may not be accepted by all schools of Islamic law). Jews generally believe that if it is possible to donate a blood or an organ to save a life, it is obligatory to do.

Part of the problem is that being born and raised in a society accustomed to the use of a seemingly endless supply of disposable products, it is quite easy to develop such ecologically unsound habits. We often lack the awareness of the impact our lifestyle has on the environment.

While perhaps the ideal Pagan would live close to the land and be conscious of how their every action effects the environment, it would be unrealistic to try to suddenly live by such a romantic goal, as we would soon become too frustrated to continue. As with any attempt to change one's attitudes and habits, true progress comes with baby steps. Instead of trying to change the world, start by sorting your trash properly if your town has a recycling program. Instead of wishing people would keep your local park clean, take a garage bag with you and donate 30 minutes to make a small dent in the mess or organize a community cleanup. Our actions may never seem heroic or significant, but any conscious effort to improve the environment is an act of devotion on a Pagan path[1].

In trying to remain aware of our actions and making the occasional sacrifice in time or convenience to do what we know is right for the environment, we have in our own way made the world a better place to live. Perhaps in time, as we begin to develop good habits and better awareness, we can extend into larger projects.

---

[1] GreenPeace.org has a great Green Guide in the "Get Involved" section of their website.

Little Things Matter!

In her book *Dreaming the Dark*, Starhawk makes a wonderful point about how the little things matter and that we can each take responsibility and make a difference, no matter how small.

While hiking along a stream with her friend they would always bring along some garbage bags to collect some of the trash they came across on their way back. Although they could not make an appreciable difference, it was enough that they made the effort to pick up any trash that lay along their path.

As a hiker, it has always been a rule of thumb to keep a small bag in my pocket for that very purpose. Even if I only walked out of the woods with one discarded can, I felt a personal sense of accomplishment and pride. It is much better than simply complaining at how people could be so rude as to toss their trash in the woods; that would only make me more bitter and chances are that trash would probably still be there!

Awareness is really key here. Learning how our daily lives impact the environment and what options are available to us allows us to begin to make changes for the better. For example, consider the debate of paper vs plastic bags when shopping. Research on the web would probably bring some conflicting studies although the general argument is that both paper and plastic bags consume large amounts of natural resources to produce and sadly the majority will eventually end up in the landfill. Paper can be recycled (consuming resources to process) or composted but plastic can be reused around the house in many ways before eventually breaking and finding its way to the landfill. However, reusable bags are ultimately the better solution, provided we are willing to sacrifice a little convenience and money for the sake of the environment.

As you discover the true scope of your environmental impact, try not to get too frustrated. The fact is, we will always have a footprint – the objective is simply to learn to soften that impact. The more we understand our options, the more informed our decisions will be. Likewise, phases like "all natural" and "green" are often hyped for the sake of marketing, but do not necessarily indicate best choices. A little research on the web on such matters goes a long way.

Craft Laws, Charters, and Etiquette

Throughout the years there have been many attempts to create a set list of laws or rules of conduct which could be universally accepted among all Wiccans, and perhaps Pagans in general. Needless to say, such attempts have always failed, and for several reasons:

- Laws do not leave room for freedom; they define straight out the *only* choice. This borders on dogmatism, which is not an aspect of Wicca's nature.

- Laws are absolute. One does not call them "laws" without implying hierarchy and authority, neither of which exists outside of each autonomous group, coven, or tradition.

- Some rules are very coven-specific and would not apply to solitaries.

- People who have proposed laws have had a tendency to include personal opinions and issues which are simply too general to be a "law" vs a friendly suggestion.

- Beliefs and practices can vary greatly between traditions. It would be nearly impossible (if possible at all) to define specific guidelines that everyone would agree upon.

Craft Laws

Back in the late 1950s/early 1960s, Gerald Gardner introduced a long list of Craft Laws in response to some contention among the members of his coven. The laws were said to have been passed down through the ages, but today most agree they were a collection of ideas from Gardner's earlier notes mixed with his personal views for the direction of his branch of Witchcraft. While some welcomed the structure, many others found them too dogmatic to be of any use in the Craft and ignored them.

Since then, many other traditions and individuals have reworked these laws in hope of establishing a common ground on which all

Witches, or at least all Wiccans, could accept as established standards. The result has been anything but successful. While some have accepted these laws in one variation or another, they provoke criticism from others.

Apart from the aversion to dogmatism which many Pagans share, such an extensive set of laws simply cannot apply to all, and always seem to contain a certain element of the personal opinions of the creator. These laws tend to get too specific and judgmental, not to mention too long, to be of much practical value. As some would joke: "The Christians only have *ten* Commandments and look at all *their* problems!"

Craft laws, therefore, have been relegated to specific traditions or covens and have never (and probably never will) speak for all Wiccans. Appendix C lists the Craft Laws as presented by Gardner for those who may wish to examine them. Modern variations can be found on the Internet.

As it stands, there are no official Craft Laws that represent Wicca or Witchcraft as a whole, and most would agree that this is a good thing. However, a standard etiquette would probably make life much easier!

Charters

Charters (or bylaws) are coven or tradition specific guidelines that do not necessarily apply to others outside of that group.

The group dynamic of each tradition or coven would make it impossible for a universal charter for all covens. Instead I propose the development of a general outline that lists the common issues a coven would face and the typical solutions that have worked in the past.[1] These solutions would be based on the experiences of earlier successes. Each group could then reword

---

[1] I welcome your thoughts on this! In fact, if enough are interested I can set up a discussion group.

the suggested solutions to best fit their situation. For example, a Dianic coven would have less emphasis on the distribution of gender than a Gardnerian coven but both would want to clearly lay out the expectations and responsibilities of their members. Some groups may want a set High Priestess while others prefer to share in the responsibility of ritual leadership. Either way is viable depending on the preferences of members in the group and the nature of the tradition. There simply is no one way to run a coven, but starting with a time-tested outline would make for a good foundation.

Some of the issues that would be dealt with in a charter include:

- Who may attend rituals. (Some covens allow guests to Sabbats but not to Esbats, etc.)

- Attendance requirements. (Many covens expect their members to attend a certain percentage of gatherings to remain an active member.)

- Coven structure, which includes any hierarchy/offices and the responsibilities of the members.

- Rules of engagement when dealing with discord among the members.

- Requirements for ritual. (What should be worn, or for that matter, not worn, in ritual.)

- Requirements to be met for various degrees and the expectations for new members.

Basically, a charter is used to maintain order in the group and to provide a common ground for all members. Traditions who have established Craft Laws would include them in their charter but must recognize that these laws are for a given tradition or group. Since traditions are rarely centrally organized such details are best defined as a tradition forms, since it will be difficult to introduce such things after the founding group has hived off into many covens.

When working with a charter it is best to avoid inconstancies. If an exception to a rule is to be made for one, it will seem unfair to others unless such exceptions are clearly outlined in the charter. For example, if the charter states that only initiated members may attend meetings, then that should be an unwavering regulation. However, adding a clause such as "...exceptions may be granted in cases where it is unanimously agreed by initiates/elders/etc" or "...the exception is for students who are reaching their time of initiation" and so on. Some groups are more sensitive about adhering to regulations than others, but it is good practice to adhere to established procedures all the same to avoid unnecessary conflicts. Similarly, it makes no sense to have something in a charter if it is not being adhered to.

Etiquette

While Craft Laws and Charters are geared for a specific group and cannot be expected to be universally accepted, there *is* the need to consider guidelines for how *anyone* would be expected to behave when attending a Wiccan social event or circle, regardless of their affiliations.

Despite the differences among traditions, there are generally *some* common expectations unofficially shared. Although most are common sense (or at least seem like common sense to the experienced), it is unfair to expect those new to the Craft to abide by them if no one has taken the time to clearly outline what they are.

Since etiquette is intended to be universal, any such guidelines would need to be general and accommodating to both Pagans and non-Pagans alike and allow a safe environment in which various traditions can interact comfortably. A common etiquette fosters a sense of community within a religion of such diverse paths. Etiquette would be non-judgmental and simply provide enough information to avoid offending others. The general rule of thumb is to remain open minded and not discount the beliefs of others that you do not agree with. But let's look more deeply into what we must consider when developing a common set of etiquette.

Some common etiquette when interacting with other Pagans includes:

- Don't touch tools or jewelry without permission since some people are very sensitive to this. (Always ask first.)

- Many wish to keep their beliefs from the public and only use a Craft name which provides them with some anonymity. Even if you know the person's real name, ask what name to use in context with the Craft. For example, "How should I refer to you?" or "Can I call you by your real name here?" (Don't assume.)

- Respect the personal space of others. When dealing with people you do not know well, it is always best to not assume anything without asking. This is especially true with physical contact. Some people are naturally flirtatious and enjoy contact, while others prefer to maintain their "personal space."

- Accept that not everyone will share your convictions and should not be judged by them. For example, if you are a strict vegetarian it is not fair to impose that lifestyle onto others and pass judgment on those who prefer to eat meat. Likewise, a hardcore feminist need not be rude to men merely because of their gender.

- Don't assume what you consider to be common sense is common knowledge. Not everyone may share your views or realize a transgression if it is not made clear.

Some common etiquette when attending ritual or organized events includes:

- Assume anything that happens in Circle should remain in that group unless you obtain permission from the leader or organizer of the event or the individual it pertains to. Respect the right for a group to maintain its secrets, be they true verbal secrets or symbolic mysteries. This is especially important when mentioning names. Not everyone wants the public to know they attended a Pagan event. (As mentioned above, make sure to ask what name they want to be referred to as in public in relation to the Craft.) Additionally, the ritual space is a place where we are given an opportunity to let go and experience the ecstasy of ritual. One should not have to worry about other participants telling outsiders how silly they looked dancing.

- No pictures should be taken without permission of those who will be in the picture, or let people know there will be pictures so as to allow them to clear out if they do not want to be included. The same goes for recording devices.

- Avoid entering or leaving a circle once it is cast. Some people are more sensitive about this than others. Even if there is no "real" damage done, those who take circle protocol seriously will take note and the interruption can throw the group energy off. Always ask beforehand how any given group prefers to work within the circle so you know how to exit properly, should it be necessary.

- Once you leave a circle, do not return unless you are needed. Exiting was one disruption, returning would be a second. If you need to exit a circle try to wait outside the perimeter until the next transition in the ritual, such as when the ritual is moving into the Cakes and Ale section. This would be less disruptive than walking back in the middle of an activity.

- Don't hold personal conversations or interrupt a ritual in progress unless it is absolutely necessary, such as to request medical attention or to alert of a robe that has caught fire. (Hey, it happens! I have seen robes, altar decorations, and even *hair* catch on fire and not be immediately noticed!) The point here is that if you are attending a ritual you are there to participate and should recognize that you are in sacred space. If this is not the case, you should not be there!

- Drugs should be kept out of public events unless organizers have approved of such things. Getting caught would cause problems not only for you but for the organizers. What you do (consensually) in the privacy of your coven or group is your own business but in public events it is the business of those who organize it. This may also include alcohol, often due to rules of the venue being used, so it is best to confirm before bringing any.

- It is considered rude to attend a ritual or event under the influence of a mind-altering substance, including alcohol. It is bad practice in general and few circles will appreciate it.

- If you don't like the way things are being done, leave and respect the right for the rest to practice in their way. If you feel that the practices are unethical, then that is a judgment call you must make. Disagreements do not always imply unethical behavior.

- Turn cell phones and pagers off unless you *must* have them on (for example, if you are a doctor on call). If they must be on, set them to vibrate instead of ring and inform the ritual leader or organizer you may need to leave if there is an emergency.

- If food will be prepared don't expect special needs to be cared for if they were never made known to the organizers. For example, a strict vegetarian attending a weekend event that includes meals should make sure the organizers are aware of their dietary needs. Likewise, when bringing food to share make sure to label clearly what is in it (meat, dairy, grains, nuts, etc). This is important not just because of dietary preference but because of food allergies.

There is also etiquette to consider for those planning or hosting a ritual or event. This is especially important when dealing with events that are open to the general public and can include those new to the Craft as well as the curious.

- Issues related to physical contact or nudity should always be made clearly known to avoid misunderstandings. Some people are not comfortable being touched, so open rituals that involve such things need to be announced.

- Always provide a nonalcoholic option for toasts or Cakes and Ale, and clearly state which is which since there may be some among us who cannot consume alcohol for various reasons which they may not want to be shared. This could be extended for dietary needs as well, either by choice (such as vegetarians) or due to health-related issues (such as diabetes or food allergies).

- For public rituals and events that will include some visitors unfamiliar to your practice, take a moment to outline the key points of ritual and what will be expected of the participants. Remember little things, like telling someone to wait until all drink and food has been distributed before partaking in the Cakes and Ale section for example, if you prefer to lead the toast.

- Any specialized requirements or guidelines need to be made clearly known if they are expected to be followed, such as any preferred ways to request exit from a circle or special restrictions such as not wearing metal or electronics like watches.

A Framework for Ethical Decision Making

As was discussed in the beginning of this discourse, the topic of ethics is not as simple as it may appear at first glance. There is no universal formula or algorithm for moral decision making since the issues must be considered in the context of the situation. Likewise, good moral decision making involves more than simply acting on hunches or intuition, although these too can play a useful role in the process.

The following guide is intended only as an aid when faced with an ethical issue. It is not a complete formula or system, and it does not guarantee good decisions. However, it can assist one in better evaluating ethical issues which can lead to more sound decisions.

1) Recognize an Ethical Issue

It may sound silly, but the first step is to know that one is facing a moral or ethical issue. Since we often react without conscious consideration, this step is all the more important.

But how does one recognize a moral issue? Common clues include conflicts between two or more values or ideals. Issues that go deeper than legal or institutional concerns may also indicate a moral issue.

2) Get All the Facts

Before we can make a sound moral decision, we first need to understand as fully as possible the nature of the problem and who or what is involved. The importance of this step cannot be stressed enough.

Here are a few questions to consider in finding the relevant facts:

- Think through the shared values that are at stake in making this decision. Is there a question of trust or fairness? Will anyone be harmed or helped?

- Who are the interested parties? Often there are more parties whose interests should be taken into consideration than is immediately obvious since they may not be directly involved. Look at the relationships between the parties, with yourself, and with relevant institutions or groups. Do some have a greater stake because they have a special need (eg, those who are poor or excluded) or because we have special obligations to them (such as children or employers)?

- What are the legal considerations and ramifications? Keep in mind organizations may also have policies or codes of ethics that must be considered. Sometimes there are bad laws, or bad rules, and sometimes those should be broken. But usually it is ethically important to pay attention to laws and rules.

- Do you feel you have enough information? If not, who can you consult?

3) Evaluate the Alternative Actions from Various Moral Perspectives

Once we know the facts and thus the context of the situation, we can weigh the benefits and the burdens. Since there are many perspectives in determining what is right or wrong, it helps to be able to relate the issue to various perspectives. We'll always have our preferences but for the sake of maintaining an open mind we must recognize that others involved may not share those perspectives.

A few things to consider during your evaluation:

- Which option will produce the most good and do the least harm?

- Which option respects the rights and dignity of all stakeholders?

- Even if not everyone gets all they want, will everyone still be treated fairly?

- Which option would promote the common good and help all participate more fully in the goals we share as a society, as a community, as a company, as a family?

- Which option would enable the deepening or development of those virtues or character traits that we value? Remember not only to consider those virtues we value as individuals but also what is valued in our profession and our society.

- Will you be compromising your own needs or rights? (Don't loose sight of your own needs. It is up you to decide when the needs of others outweigh your own, and there is no shame in choosing your own needs above those of another.)

Don't hesitate to ask others their opinion. It can be very difficult to consider every possible perspective and asking others may provide yet another way to look at the situation.

4) Make a Decision

At some point we need to stop pondering the issues and make a decision. We will not always have the luxury of time, so we must make the best of the situation and come to a decision as soon as possible.

A few things to consider in making a decision:

- Considering the various perspectives listed in the previous step, which of the options is the right thing to do?

- Are you comfortable with this decision? Sometimes your intuition will tell you if you've missed something. Would you be comfortable telling your family and friends about it? Would you want children to take your behavior as an example? Most importantly, can you live with this decision?

- Imagine discussing the situation with someone you respect. What would that person choose to do? What would that person think of your choice?

5) Act, then Reflect on the Decision Later

Once faced with an ethical decision, we cannot escape involvement. Choosing *not* to act is in itself an ethical choice and does not free us from the implications and responsibility of that choice. With that said, once we have made our decision we must follow through and take the appropriate action, even if that action is to *not* act.

The process, however, does not end with making a decision and taking action. We often learn much from the results of our decisions, and the decision making process is not perfect. We *will* make mistakes, but these mistakes are not failures unless we deny our responsibility or do not learn from them.

Some things to consider while reflecting on the outcome:

- How did it turn out for all concerned?
- Were the results as expected?
- What did you learn from the experience?
- If you had to do it over again, what, if anything, would you do differently?

Remember, making an ethical decision always carries the risk of error. We often do not know if a decision was correct until long after it has been made. The point is not so much to make the right choices (although obviously that is the goal) but rather to take the responsibility of such decisions seriously. When conflicting ethics are concerned, there is rarely a "right" answer, but in taking the responsibility to consider the issues as best possible, you can at least take comfort in knowing the decision was *justified* and not based on a whim.   Should you ultimately find yourself not satisfied with the results of your decision, you will be able to draw from that experience in the future to hopefully make a more sound decision at that time. This is truly the mark of wisdom.

The Wiccan Rede:
A Historical Journey

Today's Wiccan ethics largely center on the Wiccan Rede: *If it harms none, do what you will.* Longer versions are in circulation adding poetry or personal views (or both), but these eight words are the focal point of these variants and best sum up the nature of Wiccan ethics: to harm none.

The history of the Wiccan Rede proved more complicated to research than expected. Although by the 1980s the Rede was a standard inclusion in books on Wicca, there were very few references to it prior to the mid-1970s.[1] This may have partly been due to the fact that Wicca was primarily a secretive religion to non-initiates prior to the end of the 1960s, but also because ethics were not a topic of focus in the early years of Wicca, when more emphasis was placed on history and defining witchcraft practices. By the early 1970s both the Gardnerian and Alexandrian traditions had gained momentum, having become established in the United States, where they quickly spread. As Wicca received more public attention, and solitary practice began to explode, many public Wiccans felt the need to emphasize

---

[1] See bibliography for a list of books prior to 1980 (that I could find) that contained mention of the Rede.

Wiccan morality. In the 1980s authors such as Raymond Buckland and Scott Cunningham had introduced simplified handbooks that catered to solitary practitioners.

Another problem in researching the Rede is that books were not the only means through which information was shared. Newsletters (many with short life spans), gatherings, and by the 1980s computer bulletin board systems and the Internet all provided a means to disseminate information. Often this information lacked references and proper credit, making any attempt at accurate research daunting at best.

Oral tradition can also not be forgotten. Just as many popular chants today were introduced at pagan gatherings and passed on through other gatherings before making their way into print, many early aspects of the Craft were not necessarily formally incorporated into a book of shadows or publication right away. That which is passed on orally can easily slip into obscurity, loosing any association with the one who originated it.

This chapter will rely primarily on written resources although some first-hand accounts have helped to tie the fragments together. I welcome feedback and encourage you to share your own insights and research to help fill in the gaps.

The Early Years

In researching the origins of the Rede, I started with the works of Gerald Gardner (1884-1964). Whether or not Garner revived a dying religion or created one from scratch is not at issue here. Debates aside, Gardner was instrumental in bringing the Craft to the public and his work, and along with that of Doreen Valiente (1922-1999), became much of the foundation of what has become modern Wicca.

Keep in mind that Gardner's version of witchcraft was not the only form available. Among these variations were hereditary witches and other traditionalists, many of which did not care for the Gardnerian variety. Many of these forms of witchcraft were less religious in form, and often more intellectual in emphasis than the Gardnerian and Alexandrian varieties, which were more emotional in emphasis and made more use of chants and dancing. Sadly, many of these forms were not as visible and some who claimed to be hereditary witches were not in actuality, although it was a useful way to justify their personal practice or views, especially at a time when much emphasis and value was being placed on the perceived history of the Craft and the significance of old lineage. Modern Wicca has become such a melting pot of beliefs and the increasing sense of freedom has encouraged the sharing of ideas to such an extent that it is often quite difficult to discover their origins.

In researching Gardner's work I sought only to find mention of the Wiccan Rede, be it in context or verbatim, and if possible find earlier references. Prior to his third book, *The Meaning of Witchcraft*, published in 1959, Gardner did not discuss ethics. Even in this text, the Rede was not yet formalized as it is now, but rather it only touched upon its essence of the Wiccan ethos as "harm none."

> [Witches] are inclined to the morality of the legendary Good King Pausol [sic], "Do what you like so long as you harm no one." But they believe a certain law to be important, "You must not use magic for anything which will cause harm to anyone, and if, to prevent a greater wrong being done, you must discommode someone, you must do it only in a way which will abate the harm."[1]

Although the above quote has been cited many times in previous papers on the origin of the Rede, there was no indication of who

---

[1] Gerald Gardner, *The Meaning of Witchcraft*, page 127 in the 1982 and 1999 printings – the author is unsure about the page number of earlier copies.

this "Good King Pausol" was. It turns out that King Pausole (not "Pausol") was a literary character in the story *The Adventures of King Pausole* (1901) by Pierre Louÿs (1870-1925), a French novelist.[1]

The specific quote Gerald was referring to was:

> I. Do no wrong to thy neighbor.
> II. Observing this, do as thou pleasest.[2]

Already this has the feel of the Rede, but it had not yet been articulated in the form popular today.

The Gardnerian Craft Laws, which were introduced around 1957 and finalized around 1961, make further reference to the idea of the Rede, although again only in context: "And for long we have obeyed this law, 'Harm none.'"[3]

When associating the Rede with Gardner, most scholars suggest the Rede is actually based on the older Law of Thelema created by Aleister Crowley (1875-1947) in his work *Liber AL vel Legis* (1904), more commonly known as *The Book of the Law*.

> Who calls us Thelemites will do no wrong, if he look but close
> into the word. For there are therein Three Grades, the Hermit,
> and the Lover, and the man of Earth. Do what thou wilt shall
> be the whole of the Law.[4]

---

[1] It is rather ironic that Gardner, who was often accused of mixing his own sexual tastes into Wiccan practice (such as working skyclad and the use of the scourge in initiation) would specifically site Louÿs as the basis of a witch's morality, since Louÿs was well known for the erotic nature of his work. I bring this up more for the humor than as an accusation. Regardless of Gardner's intentions, his work was instrumental in bringing Wicca to life as a viable modern religion. For more information on the literary character King Pausole, see Appendix B.

[2] Pierre Louÿs, *Collected Works of Pierre Louÿs*, 1932, page 321.

[3] Kelly, Aidan , Public contents of the Gardnerian Book of Shadows (sacred-texts.com), "The Old Laws (1961)" or Kelly, Aidan, *Crafting the Art of Magic: Book 1*, 1991, page 159.

[4] Aleister Crowley, *The Book of the Law*, Chapter 1, verse 40.

Even among the Ordo Templi Orientis (OTO), an outer Thelemic order, there is some debate on the interpretation of this phrase, but those who connect it with the Rede tend to feel that "harm none" is implied from the context of the believed source of Crowley's inspiration; Francois Rabelais' novel *Gargantua* published in 1534.

> DO AS THOU WILT because men that are free, of gentle birth, well bred and at home in civilized company possess a natural instinct that inclines them to virtue and saves them from vice. This instinct they name their honor.[1]

To be more precise, the text that would later become the *Book of the Law* was said to have been dictated to Crowley from a being called *Aiwass*, an angel of the highest order. However, in 1920, when Crowley set up his establishment in Sicily, he called it the Abbey of Thelema, which is also taken from Rabelais, and in his book *Magick in Theory and Practice*, the works of Francois Rabelais were recommended for its invaluable wisdom. So Crowley was indeed familiar with the work of Rabelais.

Although the extent of influence on the Rede is debatable, Crowley's influence cannot be easily dismissed. Gardner was initiated into the OTO by Crowley in 1946 and was rumored to have met with Crowley as far back as 1936. After Crowley's death in 1947, many regarded Gerald as an obvious successor as leader of the order, especially since he had been granted (purchased) a charter by Crowley empowering Gardner to start a local encampment of the order. Therefore, Gardner was more than just slightly involved with the OTO and its teachings. Being that other writings of Gardner, such as the Charge of the Goddess, were reworked by Doreen Valiente since, as she put it: "People are just not going to accept this and take it seriously so long as they think you're an offshoot of Crowley's OTO[2]", it is quite possible that she also encouraged Gardner to keep the Rede away from

---

[1] Francois Rabelais, *Gargantua*, 1534.
[2] Doreen Valiente, 1991 interview with *FireHeart* Journal.

sounding like a work of Crowley. Valiente, an early initiate and High Priestess of Gardner considered by many to be the "mother of Wicca" for her significant influence in Gardner's work, was entrusted with editing Gardner's notes into a more formal book of shadows.

As will be discussed in the next section, Doreen Valiente was no stranger to the writings of Crowley. In relating Crowley's work with Wiccan ethics, Valiente also reminds us that the concept of following one's will is nothing new:

> The teachings of Crowley's, embodied in the dictum quoted above, "Do what thou wilt," is by no means new, and was not invented by him. Long ago, Saint Augustine said, "Love and do what you will". The initiate of ancient Egypt declared: "There is no part of me that is not of the gods." The pagan Greeks originated the saying: "To the pure all things are pure." The implication is that when one has reached a high state of spiritual development and evolution one has passed beyond the comparatively petty rules of religion and society at some particular time and place, and may indeed do what one wills, because one's true will is then knowable, and must of its own nature be right. The Upanishads or sacred scriptures of ancient India tell us that the knower of Brahma is beyond both good and evil.[1]

Eight Words...

The first recorded mention of the Wiccan Rede in the eight-word form popular today, at least that I have been able to discover thus far, was in a speech by Doreen Valiente on October 3, 1964, at what may have been the first witches' dinner organized in modern history. The event was sponsored by *Pentagram*, a quarterly newsletter and "witchcraft review" started and published by Gerard Noel in 1964.

---

[1] Doreen Valiente, *Witchcraft for Tomorrow*, 1978, page 44.

> Demanding tolerance between covens as well as toward the outside world, Doreen spoke the Anglo-Saxon witch formula called the *Wiccan Rede* or wise teaching: "Eight words the Wiccan Rede fulfil, An' it harm none, do what ye will."[1]

The above quote is from Hans Holzer's book, *The Truth About Witchcraft*, first published in 1969 and again in 1971. This was one of the first books to present witchcraft from an outsider's view[2] looking in, observing some of the practices of the various forms of witchcraft in both the US and UK around at the time.

Valiente's "Eight Words" quote was also published in volume one of the *Pentagram* (1964), the UK newsletter that hosted the event and as will be discussed later was subsequently published between circa 1965 and 1966 in the United States in *The Waxing Moon* newsletter. In 1965 the Rede was again quoted without references in Justine Glass' book, *Witchcraft, The Sixth Sense*:

> The other, only slightly less important belief of the witches is in hurtlessness; an article of faith also of the ancient Huna religion, which is thought to have originated in Africa and traveled across the world, by way of Egypt and India to Hawaii. The kahunas taught that the only sin was to hurt – either oneself or someone else. The Wiccan Rede (ie Counsel or advice of the Wise Ones) is: "An ye harm no one, do what ye will."[3]

Sadly no reference is given but since Glass had quoted from *Pentagram* earlier in that chapter, it is quite possible that her above mention of the Rede derived from something inspired by Valiente's speech in 1964. The wording is a bit different from that speech, but this may have been due to the usual changes that occur when information is passed via word of mouth or as the author recalled the quote from memory. Since Glass had an advertisement calling for help in her research which was printed

---

[1] Hans Holzer, *The Truth about Witchcraft*, 1971, page 128.
[2] Although he himself was involved in the Craft.
[3] Justine Glass, *Witchcraft, The Sixth Sense*, 1965, page 58.

in the same issue of *Pentagram* (and on the very same page) as Valiente's "Eight Words" quote, this is a likely source.

Glass' book also goes on to discuss how one of the coven's duties is to keep its members in check when emotions are strong. This ethical support mentality was also mentioned by Gardner in *The Meaning of Witchcraft*, as well as other authors in the 1970s. As I will discuss in the chapter on the Three-fold Law, as traditional covens gave way to solitary practice (for the majority), something was needed to fill in for the coven's grounding element to provide "moral restraint." This replacement was the emphasis on the Wiccan Rede and the Three-fold Law. As Glass insinuated, ethics was not a significant focus in the Craft at the time (around 1965), although the idea of harming none was generally accepted.

Another interesting variation is mentioned by Dr. Leo Louis Martello (1930-2000) in his book *Witchcraft: The Old Religion* (first published in 1973): "Witch credo 'And ye harm none do what thou wilt.'"[1] According to Dr. Martello, the quote was part of an article dated March 15, 1972 in *The Villanovan*, the newspaper of the Students Union of the Catholic Villanova University in Pennsylvania, USA. Again, no sources were given. Thanks to a Pagan employee at Villanova University I was able to obtain the article, which was actually dated March 22, 1972. While I do not have a full transcript of the lecture, the article itself only briefly mentions that the "power (of witchcraft) is not used for evil purposes."[2] It then quotes a variation of the three-fold law.

Circa 1970/1971, Alex Sanders (1926-1988) composed a series of lectures written by himself and others which were privately distributed as a course for novices in Alexandrian Wicca, a tradition Sanders founded. In the essay entitled, *The Book of Shadows*, the following occurs during first degree initiation:

---

[1] Dr. Leo Louis Martello, *Witchcraft: The Old Religion*, 1975, page 42.
[2] Fields, Essie, "Witches' Liberation Advocate Dispells [sic] Popular Black Magic Myths," *The Villanovan*, March 22, 1972.

> The Book [of Shadows] is closed in front of him [the one being initiated] and he is shown the cover, on which is often written the motto of Wicca: "An it harm none – do what ye will."[1]

These lectures were published in the book, *The Alex Sanders Lectures* in 1984 but were in private circulation since the 1970s. This is the only reference to the wording of the Rede in Sander's published material, although he had made reference to Crowley's "Do what thou wilt" phrase in Stewart Farrar's *What Witches Do* (1971).

When it comes to the origin of the Alexandrian tradition of Wicca, there is much controversy. Alex claimed to have been initiated into the Craft by his grandmother at the age of seven, which was later determined to be a hoax. There is also much debate as to how he was able to obtain a copy of the Gardnerian Book of Shadows, which he had passed off as his own while incorporating additional elements of ritual magic into it. The point to be made here is simply that Sander's teachings were heavily influenced by Gardner's work, among others, and that this reference to a witches' motto may have derived from Valiente's Rede assuming the wording in the lecture was not altered at a later date prior to its compilation and publishing in 1984 – long after the Rede's widespread dissemination.

There is, however, another important source for the Wiccan Rede, which is often attributed as the source of its origins. In the Ostara 1975 (Vol. III, No. 69) issue of *Green Egg* magazine, in an article called "Wiccan-Pagan Potpourri," was a long (but most will find very familiar) poem called the *Rede Of The Wiccae*:

Rede Of The Wiccae

Being known as the counsel of the Wise Ones:

1. Bide the Wiccan laws ye must,
   in perfect love and perfect trust.

---

[1] Baker, J. (ed.), *The Alex Sanders Lectures*, 1984, page 67.

2. Live an let live –
   fairly take an' fairly give.

3. Cast the Circle thrice about
   To keep all evil spirits out.

4. To bind the spell every time,
   let the spell be spake in rhyme.

5. Soft of eye an light of touch –
   speak little, listen much.

6. Deosil go by the waxing Moon –
   sing an dance the Wiccan rune.

7. Widdershins go when the Moon doth wane,
   an the Werewolf howls by the dread Wolfsbane.

8. When the Lady's Moon is new,
   kiss thy hand to her times two.

9. When the Moon rides at her peak,
   then your heart's desire seek.

10. Heed the Northwind's mighty gale –
    lock the door and drop the sail.

11. When the wind comes from the South,
    love will kiss thee on the mouth.

12. When the wind blows from the East,
    expect the new and set the feast.

13. When the West wind blows o'er thee,
    departed spirits restless be.

14. Nine woods in the Cauldron go –
    burn them quick an' burn them slow.

15. Elder be ye Lady's tree –
    burn it not or cursed ye'll be.

16. When the Wheel begins to turn –
    let the Beltane fires burn.

17. When the Wheel has turned a Yule,
    light the Log an let Pan rule.

18. Heed ye flower bush an tree –
    by the Lady blessed be.

19. Where the rippling waters go,
    cast a stone an truth ye'll know.

20. When ye have need,
    hearken not to other's greed.

21. With the fool no season spend
    or be counted as his friend.

22. Merry meet an merry part –
    bright the cheeks an warm the heart.

23. Mind the Threefold Law ye should –
    three times bad an three times good.

24. When misfortune is enow,
    wear the blue star on thy brow.

25. True in love ever be
    unless thy lover's false to thee.

26. Eight words the Wiccan Rede fulfill –
    an it harm none, do what ye will.[1]

Lady Gwen Thomson[2] (1928-1986), a hereditary witch from New Haven, Connecticut (USA), attributed this text to Adriana Porter[3] (1857-1946), her paternal grandmother, who, as she stated "was well into her 90s when she crossed over into the Summerlands in 1946."[4] Thomson was the primary teacher of The New England Coven of the Traditionalist Witches (NECTW), which she founded in 1972, although her teachings were brought to the

---

[1] *Green Egg* magazine, Vol. III. No. 69 (Ostara 1975).
[2] Later known as Lady Gwynne.
[3] For more on Adriana Porter and Lady Gwen Thomson see *The Rede of the Wiccae* by Robert Mathiesen and Theitic. Thetic is an elder in Thomson's tradition.
[4] New England Coven of the Traditionalist Witches website.

public in the late 1960s. This tradition was a combination of her family's tradition blended with popular occultism. This was the first time the Rede was publicly referred to as a "rede" (guideline) since Valiente's 1964 speech and subsequent mention in the *Pentagram* and *The Waxing Moon*, and although the line numbers never quite took hold, the text itself did, especially the last line. This is also the first time the Rede was introduced in such a visible and easily distributed manner and at a time when the Craft was blossoming in creativity and public interest.

Joseph B. Wilson[1] (1942-2004), publisher of the first witchcraft newsletter in the United States, *The Waxing Moon*, and who for many years acted as a central networking hub for correspondence, contacts, etc, shared with me that Lady Gwen was one of his early correspondents. Although Wilson could not remember much about her, he recalled that he shared a good bit of his own information from his mentors with her – which by some accounts has since ended up as part of her adapted hereditary lineage. Mr. Wilson was also able to confirm two other important links to Valiente's Rede influence on the Porter/Thomson Rede:

1) Wilson clearly remembers reprinting Valiente's words in *The Waxing Moon*. Since his archive was lost several years ago, he could not give an exact date, but it would have been circa 1965-1966.

2) Gwen Thompson was a subscriber to *The Waxing Moon*.

Although this offers some links to a possible influence of Valiente's Rede in the development of Lady Gwen's rede, it is not conclusive and so we are left with three likely scenarios:

---

[1] I am indebted to Tori McElroy for contacting me in reference to an early version of this paper and bringing me in contact with Mr. Wilson, and grateful to Mr. Wilson for sharing with me scanned copies of the issues of *Pentagram*, which incidentally, is why you can now find the whole set circulating online. We each exchanged scans of the issues we had and he later made them available to the public via his website before his death.

A) Lady Gwen's stated history of her version of the Rede is accurate and was written by her grandmother. This will raise the question: If the passing of Adriana Porter came before the publishing of Gardner's first book, which contained elements of witchcraft ritual (*High Magic's Aid*, 1949), and after Gardner is said to have been initiated by "Old Dorothy Clutterbuck" in 1939, then could they share a common source? Or could one have perhaps inspired the Rede from the other? I could find no evidence to support or deny this.

B) Lady Gwen adapted a poem written by her grandmother, adding more Wiccan-like elements. Since the tradition Lady Gwen taught is freely described as an adaptation of her hereditary tradition, it is quite possible that Valiente's Rede influenced some of the rewording of Adriana Porter's original poem, perhaps even unconsciously doing so.

C) The entire history of Lady Gwen's Rede was made up to add a sense of lineage and credibility to her established tradition. The questionable claims of family-based initiations pre-dating Gardner were not uncommon and readily abused, so the accuracy of Thomson's claim will always remain somewhat debatable without documentation.

By 1978 in her book *Witchcraft for Tomorrow*, Doreen Valiente had also mentioned the Wiccan Rede.

> This idea has been put into a rhymed couplet called the Wiccan Rede:
>
>> Eight Words the Wiccan Rede fulfil:
>> An it harm none, do what ye will.
>
> This can be expressed in more modern English as follows:

Eight words the Witches' Creed fulfil:
If it harms none, do what you will.[1]

Later in the same book, a longer poetic version of the Rede that Valiente called the *Witches' Creed* was introduced.[2]

The Witches' Creed

Hear now the words of the witches,
The secrets we hid in the night,
When dark was our destiny's pathway,
That now we bring forth into light.

Mysterious water and fire,
The earth and the wide-ranging air,
By hidden quintessence we know them,
And will and keep silent and dare.

The birth and rebirth of all nature,
The passing of winter and spring,
We share with the life universal,
Rejoice in the magical ring.

Four times in the year the Great Sabbat
Returns, and witches are seen
At Lammas and Candlemas dancing,
On May Eve and old Hallowe'en.

When day-time and night-time are equal,
When the sun is at greatest and least,
The four Lesser Sabbats are summoned,
Again witches gather in feast.

Thirteen silver moons in a year are,
Thirteen is the coven's array.
Thirteen times as Esbat make merry,
For each golden year and a day.

---

[1] Doreen Valiente, *Witchcraft for Tomorrow*, 1978, page 41.

[2] I found a similar untitled poem © 1974 by Doreen Valiente in *Earth Religion News* Volume 3 Issues 1, 2, & 3 combined (1976) which ends with the same four lines as the Witches' Creed found in *Witchcraft for Tomorrow*. It looks like an earlier longer draft with many of the same quartets but in a different order.

The power was passed down the ages,
Each time between woman and man,
Each century unto the other,
Ere time and the ages began.

When drawn is the magical circle,
By sword or athame or power,
Its compass between the two worlds lie,
In Land of the Shades for that hour.

This world has no right then to know it,
And world beyond will tell naught,
The oldest of Gods are invoked there,
The Great Work of magic is wrought.

For two are the mystical pillars,
That stand to at the gate of the shrine,
And two are the powers of nature,
The forms and the forces divine.

The dark and the light in succession,
The opposites each unto each,
Shown forth as a God and a Goddess,
Of this did our ancestors teach.

By night he's the wild wind's rider,
The Horn'd One, the Lord of the shades,
By day he's the King of the Woodlands,
The dweller in green forest glades.

She is youthful or old as she pleases,
She sails the torn clouds in her barque,
The bright silver lady of midnight,
The crone who weaves spells in the dark.

The master and mistress of magic,
They dwell in the deeps of the mind,
Immortal and ever-renewing,
With power to free or to bind.

So drink the good wine to the Old Gods,
And dance and make love in their praise,
Til Elphame's fair land shall receive us,
In peace at the end of our days.

An Do What You Will be the challenge,
So be it in Love that harms none,
For this is the only commandment,
By Magick of old, be it done.[1]

Often the "eight words" couplet is tacked on to this when quoted by others, but in *Witchcraft for Tomorrow*, where the Witches' Creed was introduced as part of the Sabbat Rite, only the above text was read after forming the circle. The "eight words" couplet was used separately in the same ritual, following the reading of the longer Creed text.

> Then take up the pentacle, and pass deosil with it round the circle, holding it up at the four quarters, east, south, west and north, and repeating each time:
>
> > Eight words the Witches' Creed fulfil:
> > If it harms none, do what you will.[2]

So technically the "eight words" couplet poetically refers to the Crede and is not part of the long version of Creed itself, since that already includes a similar couplet:

> An Do What You Will be the challenge,
> So be it in Love that harms none.

This is a minor point, and the long Creed can of course be used either way, but for the sake of accuracy I wanted to make the clarification.

Valiente's earlier book, *An ABC of Witchcraft Past & Present*, which was first published in 1973, had no specific entry for the Rede, despite introducing it in her 1964 speech. Chances are it had not yet "taken hold" in the early Wiccan "community" that was still largely segregated and coven-centric by 1973, and thus was not yet something established enough to be included in an encyclopedia of witchcraft. However, in the entry on Basic Beliefs

---

[1] Doreen Valiente, *Witchcraft for Tomorrow*, 1978, page 72.
[2] Doreen Valiente, *Witchcraft for Tomorrow*, 1978, page 74.

of Witches, a variation of the Rede was mentioned as part of the discourse on the Witches' ethics:

> Witches do not believe that true morality consists of observing a list of thou-shalt-nots. Their morality can be summed up in one sentence, "Do what you will, so long as it harms none." This does not mean, however, that witches are pacifists. They say that to allow wrong to flourish unchecked is *not* 'harming none.' On the contrary, it is harming everybody.[1]

This is a perfect example of the perception of Wiccan ethics prior to the 1980s. Witches were not the epitome of light and love but rather real people who dealt with real situations, not afraid to get their hands dirty when necessary. Witches had a respect for life that was balanced with both its nurturing aspects and the harsh reality of the fight for survival. The Rede was a summary or point of reference, but not a complete ethical system in itself.

If the Rede (or at least a version of it) was written by Valiente, then the Crowley influence needs to be accepted as possibility. While Gardner does not associate Crowley with Wiccan ethics despite drawing from Crowley's work in other areas, Doreen Valiente, a poet at heart, would have been much more open to using Crowley's Law.

> And mind you, Aleister Crowley, in my opinion, was a marvelous poet and he has always been undervalued in English literature simply because of the notoriety which he made for himself and reveled in. He loved being called the wickedest man in the world and all that sort of nonsense. The thing is – as his latest biographer, John Symonds, says – he couldn't have it both ways. If he wanted to get himself that lurid reputation, which he worked very hard at for many years, then he wasn't, at the same time, going to get a good reputation in English literature, in spite of the fact that a couple of his poems are in The Oxford Book of English Mystical Verse. I think it's a pity that he's not had the

---

[1] Doreen Valiente, *An ABC of Witchcraft Past & Present*, 1973, page 55.

recognition that he deserves, really, and perhaps later years will remedy that.[1]

Many of Doreen's books mentioned Crowley and recognized his indirect influence in Wiccan beliefs and practices. Even in the long text of Valiente's Creed listed above, there is a line that is very reminiscent of Crowley's dictum "Love is the Law, Love under Will" that traditionally followed the greeting "Do what thou wilt shall be the whole of the Law." Even the spelling of "magick" with a K in the last line of Valiente's Creed is also very characteristic of Thelema.

> An Do What You Will be the challenge,
> So be it in Love that harms none,
> For this is the only commandment,
> By Magick of old, be it done.

By the 1980s, most books made reference to the Rede, sometimes modernizing it and other times making it more archaic sounding. By the 1990s many were clueless of the Rede's history and several new variations of the Rede, often anonymous or lacking references, were scattered throughout newsletters and of course over the Internet. More variants seem to use the Porter/Thompson version of the Rede, including catch phrases such as "in perfect love and perfect trust"[2] and "merry ye meet, and merry ye part," which are specific to it. It should be noted however, that the phrase "in perfect love and perfect trust" is also found in the (publicly known) first-degree Gardnerian initiation rituals.[3]

---

[1] Doreen Valiente, 1991 interview with *FireHeart* Journal.

[2] The phase "in perfect love and perfect trust" was in use by other traditions long before the printing of the Rede Of The Wiccae in the Ostara 1975 *Green Egg*.

[3] Aidan Kelly traces this back to 1949 in *Crafting the Art of Magic: Book 1*, page 55. See also the Public Contents of the Gardnerian Book of Shadows (sacred-texts.com), "The Initiation (1949)."

Rede Timeline

Below is a quick timeline for various sources, inspirations, or appearances of the Rede or related events. Although I have a rather extensive library, I am sure I am missing some early books and newsletters that may help fill in the gaps. I consider this book a "work in progress" and encourage you to contact me[1] if you have any information to share. Please keep in mind, however, that I need to be able to confirm the sources to ensure accuracy although I also welcome first hand experiences, if only to lead me to new material.

Note: First Publication dates given for all books unless otherwise noted.

Date	Source	Quote/Notes
1534	Francois Rabelais' novel *Gargantua*	"DO AS THOU WILT because men that are free, of gentle birth, well bred and at home in civilized company possess a natural instinct that inclines them to virtue and saves them from vice. This instinct they name their honor." (Crowley's Inspiration)
1901	Pierre Louÿs's *The Adventures of King Pausole* (English version in 1919)	I. Do no wrong to thy neighbor. II. Observing this, do as thou pleasest. (Gardner's Inspiration)
1904	Crowley's *The Book of the Law*	"Do what thou wilt shall be the whole of the Law." (Possible influence on Gardner and others familiar with OTO or Crowley)

---

[1] Visit JohnCoughlin.com for my current contact information.

1946	(various sources)	Adriana Porter, who is said to have written the version of the Rede printed in 1975 in *Green Egg*, dies.
1952-1953	Doreen Valiente's *The Rebirth of Witchcraft*	Doreen Valiente meets (1952) and is initiated (1953) by Gardner. (If Valiente did not write Rede, any sources could possibly predate this time.)
1956	Gerald Gardner's *The Meaning of Witchcraft*	"[Witches] are inclined to the morality of the legendary Good King Pausol [sic], "Do what you like so long as you harm no one." (This is the first book on "modern" witchcraft to cite the ethics of witchcraft.)
1957-1961	The Old Laws, Gerald Gardner's Gardnerian (public) Book of Shadows: (Section D.1)	"And for long we have obeyed this law, 'Harm none'" (Reflect general consensus that Witches did not tend to have a desire to cause harm.)
1964	(various sources)	Gerald Gardner dies.
1964	Doreen Valiente's Speech	"Eight words the Wiccan Rede fulfil, An' it harm none, do what ye will." (First time Rede as we know it today mentioned publicly?)
1964	*Pentagram* newsletter published by Gerard Noel in the UK	"Eight words the Wiccan Rede fulfil, An' it harm none, do what ye will."

1965	Justine Glass' *Witchcraft, The Sixth Sense*	"The Wiccan Rede (ie Counsel or advice of the Wise Ones) is: 'An ye harm no one, do what ye will.'" Note wording is different. (First book I have found to mention the Rede.)
circa 1965-66	*The Waxing Moon* newsletter published by Joseph B. Wilson in the USA	Joseph Wilson clearly remembers reprinting Valiente's words in *The Waxing Moon*, but he could not give an exact date as sadly his archive had been lost several years ago.
1967	Patricia Crowther quote in *Witchraft in the World Today*, by C.H. Wallace	"Harm no one, have perfect love and perfect trust."
1969 and 1971	Hans Holzer's *The Truth About Witchcraft*	Mentioned Doreen Valiente's 1964 Speech and quotes the Rede. "Eight words the Wiccan Rede fulfil, An' it harm none, do what ye will." (Although this book is now out of print and lost popularity as Wicca became more publicly known, this was the first book to give insight into the various types of modern witches at a time when this information was not widely available, and peaked much interest in the public.)
Circa 1970 to 1971	Alex Sander's lecture on the Book of Shadows	"The motto of Wicca: 'An it harm none – do what ye will." (This could have influenced early Alexandrians and possibly others.)

1972	Dr. Leo Louis Martello, *Black Magic, Satanism, and Voodoo*, quoting issue number 19 (March 1971) of *The Wiccan*	"Witches' Code – 'Harm None.'"
1973	Doreen Valiente's *An ABC of Witchcraft Past and Present*	"[Witches'] morality can be summed up in one sentence, 'Do what you will, so long as it harms none.'"
1973	Dr. Leo Louis Martello, *Witchcraft: The Old Religion*	"Witch credo 'And ye harm none do what thou wilt.'"
1973	Aricle *Witchcraft – Wisecraft – Wicca* in *Quest* issue number 15 (September 1973) written anonymously as "a First Degree Initiate"	"The code of the witches is 'Perfect Love – Perfect Trust – Harm No One'." (While not stated the content of the article leans toward the author being of a Gardnerian tradition.)
1973	Ann Grammary's *The Witch's Workbook*	"The Credo of the Witch or Wizard is AN IT HARM NONE, DO WHAT THOU WILT!"
1973	Patricia Crowther's *Witch Blood!* (autobiography quoting Gardner during her initiation which took place on June 6, 1960[1])	"Remember always to live up to the witches creed – 'Perfect love and perfect trust, ' and 'If it harms no one, do what thou wilt.'"

---

[1] The book itself did not note the date but other sources, including *The Encyclopedia of Witches & Witchcraft* by Rosemary Ellen Guiley filled in the blank.

1975	Lady Gwen Thompson, *Green Egg* magazine, Vol. III. No. 69 (Ostara 1975)	Last line of her Rede Of The Wiccae: "26. Eight words the Wiccan Rede fulfill – an it harm none, do what ye will." (This was the most visible appearance of the Rede to date.)
1976	Doreen Valiente's untitled poem © 1974	Last quartet: "An Do What You Will be the challenge, So be it in Love that harms none, For this is the only commandment, By Magick of old, be it done."
1978	Doreen Valiente's *Witchcraft for Tomorrow*	"Eight Words the Wiccan Rede fulfil: An it harm none, do what ye will. This can be expressed in more modern English as follows: Eight words the Witches' Creed fulfil: If it harms none, do what you will." Longer poem, the Witches' Creed also introduced which ends with "An Do What You Will be the challenge, So be it in Love that harms none." (First book by a well established Witch to print the Rede?)

Conclusion

I must admit I had hoped to find a simple and clean historical path for the Rede when I first began my research. Chances are Doreen Valiente, who had edited much of Gardner's work, came up with the Rede using Gardner's material. I am doubtful, however, that Gardner actually wrote the Rede himself. Although "harm none" is mentioned several times in the Craft Laws released by Gardner around 1961, the only reason given is that any harm could be blamed on witches and thus encourage further witch hunts.[1]

> But when one of our oppressors die, or even be sick, ever is the cry, "This be Witches Malice," and the hunt is up again. And though they slay ten of their people to one of ours, still they care not; they have many thousands, while we are few indeed. So it is Aredan that none shall use the Art in any way to do ill to any, however much they have injured us. And for long we have obeyed this law, "Harm none" and now times many believe we exist not. So it be Aredan that this law shall still continue to help us in our plight. No one, however great an injury or injustice they receive may use the Art in any to do ill or harm any.[2]

Not once do the laws say to harm no one because it is wrong! Likewise if there had been a standard ethical stance in the Craft, why were there no specifics in the public contents of the Gardnerian Book of Shadows? I doubt it was withheld due to secrecy given that an entire section is dedicated to the importance of working skyclad, a much more risqué topic to make public than a simple ethical statement.

However, the version of the Rede by Adriana Porter – if Thomson's claim is true – would have had to have been written before Porter's death in 1946. Although I could find no mention of it prior to its 1975 debut in *Green Egg*, that does not discount the *possibility* that it was in private circulation much earlier and that such a copy had inspired Valiente's 1964 speech.

Sadly, Gardner, Valiente, Porter, and Thomson have all passed on, leaving these questions largely unanswerable. Despite the fuzzy history of the Wiccan Rede, one thing is certain; as Wicca became more readily available, the Rede took a prominent – and

---

[1] The laws were said to be "of old" and so reflected the mentality of witches during the time of the witch persecutions. The validity of these origins, however, is debatable.
[2] Kelly, Aidan, Public contents of the Gardnerian Book of Shadows (sacred-texts.com), "The Old Laws (1961)," starting at [L:40] or Kelly, Aidan, *Crafting the Art of Magic: Book 1*, 1991, page 156.

needed – place in Wiccan literature. As more and more solitaries and non-traditionalists began to practice the Craft without formal initiations, the Rede ensured that the essence of Wiccan ethics was fostered and a core belief in a very open and flexible religion was established.

Today much emphasis is placed on the Rede, Karma, and the Three-fold law, sometimes to the point of fundamentalism. Perhaps since the majority of Wiccans came from predominantly Christian backgrounds, we needed the comforting structure of the moral rules we were used (conditioned?) to, or perhaps our constant battle with the public to reclaim the term "witch" from its negative stereotype forced us to begin to over emphasize our morality in hopes of placating those who would subdue us. Going back to the King Pausole reference in *The Meaning of Witchcraft*, Gardner stated that witches were *inclined* to a morality of harm none, not that they were *bound* to it. Today the Rede is often elevated to the status of law.

I am not going to attempt to analyze the meaning of the Rede itself in this chapter. I have always considered ethics to be a personal matter, not one to be tainted with a social, political, or religious agenda. This is why I like the use of the word "rede"; it infers a guideline, not a strict law, thus allowing each of us to seek our own meaning based on our own experiences, and learned by our own mistakes.

As I mentioned earlier, despite all the research, I consider this a work in progress and invite you to contact me if you feel you have any reference material or firsthand experience to add. I know, for instance, that Hans Holzer had published an article on Witchcraft prior to 1969 that was published in over 150 newspapers throughout the US. I do not know if the Rede or ethics was mentioned in that article. Likewise, there were many small newsletters and journals that came and went in both the US and UK during the 1960s and 1970s which may have disseminated the Rede, not to mention articles by early prominent authors and teachers that may have appeared in local newspapers.

On my History and Evolution of Wiccan Ethics website[1] I have added a section to include related commentary so that you may view both feedback and criticism of this site as well as further insights from visitors. I have also created a link page to list other related sites as well as on-line source material.

Bibliography

Publications referenced in this chapter:

Baker, J. (ed.). The Alex Sanders Lectures. New York: Magickal Childe, 1984.

Crow, W.B. Witchcraft, Magic & Occultism. California: Wilshire Book Company, 1968.

Crowley, Aleister. Magick in Theory and Practice. New York: Dover, 1976.

Crowther, Patricia. Witch Blood! New York: House of Collectibles, 1974.

Fields, Essie. "Witches' Liberation Advocate Dispells [sic] Popular Black Magic Myths." The Villanovan March 22, 1972.

Gardner, Gerald. Meaning of Witchcraft. New York: Magickal Childe, 1982.

Glass, Justine. Witchcraft, The Sixth Sense. London: Wilshire Book Co., 1965.

Grammary, Ann. The Witch's Workbook. New York: Pocket Books, 1973.

---

[1] Available at www.waningmoon.com/ethics.

Green, Marian (ed.). Quest No 15, September 1973.

Guiley, Rosemary Ellen. The Encyclopedia of Witches & Witchcraft – second edition. New York: Checkmark Books, 1999.

Holzer, Hans. The Truth About Witchcraft. New York: Pocket Book, 1971.

Holzer, Hans. The Witchcraft Report. New York: Ace, 1973.

Hymenaeus Beta X° (ed.). The Equinox Vol III, No 10. Maine: Samuel Weiser, 1986.

Hutton, Ronald. The Triumph of the Moon. New York: Oxford University Press, 1999.

Kelly, Aidan. Crafting the Art of Magic: Book 1. Minnesota: Llewellyn Publications, 1991.

Louÿs, Pierre. Collected Works of Pierre Louÿs. New York: Liveright Publishing, 1932.

Martello, Dr. Leo Louis. Black Magic, Satanism, and Voodoo. New York: HC Publishers, 1972.

Martello, Dr. Leo Louis. Witchcraft: The Old Religion. New Jersey: Citadel Books, 1975.

Noel, Gerard (ed.). Pentagram No. 2, November 1964.

Rabelais, Francois. Gargantua and Pantagruel. New York: Everyman's Library, 1994.

Slater, Herman (ed.). Earth Religion News Vol 3, No 1, 2 & 3 combined, 1976.

Valiente, Doreen. An ABC of Witchcraft Past and Present. New York: St. Martin's Press, 1973.

Valiente, Doreen. The Rebirth of Witchcraft. Washington: Phoenix Publishing, 1989.

Valiente, Doreen. Witchcraft for Tomorrow. Washington: Phoenix Publishing, 1978.

Wallace, C.H. Witchcraft in the World Today. New York: Award Books, 1967.

Zell-Ravenheart, Oberon (ed.). Green Egg Vol. III No 69, Ostara 1975.

Online Documents referenced in this Chapter[1]:

Public Contents of the Gardnerian Book of Shadows (Compiled from Kelly, Aidan, Crafting the Art of Magic: Book 1): www.sacred-texts.com/pag/gbos

Doreen Valiente 1991 Interview with FireHeart: www.earthspirit.com/fireheart/fhdv1.html

Doreen Valiente 1997 speech at National Conference of the Pagan Federation: users.drak.net/Lilitu/valiente.htm

New England Coven of Traditionalist Witches: www.nectw.org

Private Correspondences:

Theitic (NECTW), August 2001

Tori McElroy/Joseph B. Wilson, December 1, 2001

Tori McElroy/Joseph B. Wilson, December 3, 2001

---

[1] As of July 2009 some of these links no longer exist but the saved text can be viewed at www.waningmoon.com/ethics/sources.

The Three-Fold Law

Three-fold Law, or Law of Return as it is also called, is perhaps one of the more controversial aspects of Wiccan ethics. The basic premise is that anything we do comes back to us in the end, often to a greater degree (such as three-fold). If we do good, then good will be retuned, and if we cause harm, we put ourselves in danger of harm. Ethically it is equivalent to the Golden Rule: "Do unto others as you would have done to you." But in the case of the Law of Return, there is a literal reward or punishment tied to one's actions, particularly when it comes to working magic.

The debate over the validity of the Law of Return and its variations takes many forms. Some feel that it was created to keep new initiates in check as they learned to work with magic, while others feel it is a remnant of Christian thinking, being that a majority of Wiccans come from a Christian background. However, many Wiccans today, including some authors and "community leaders," take the three-fold law quite literally.

Since the idea that we reap what we sow is generally accepted among Wiccans, the Law of Return can fairly be considered a core belief. However, it must be acknowledged that it is neither a necessary nor a universally-defining belief of the Craft. There are many Wiccans, experienced and new alike, who view the Law of

Return as an over-elaboration on the Wiccan Rede, which recommends that we refrain from causing harm. A Wiccan would not wish to cause harm since he or she *deems it wrong* to do so, not out of fear of retribution.

Doreen Valiente, one of the most influential and respected figures in modern witchcraft, boldly stated in her speech at the National Conference of the Pagan Federation in November 1997:

> Another teaching of Gerald's which I have come to question is the belief known popularly as "The Law of Three." This tells us that whatever you send out in witchcraft you get back threefold, for good or ill.
>
> Well, I don't believe it! Why should we believe that there is a special Law of Karma that applies only to witches? For Goddess' sake do we really kid ourselves that we are that important? Yet I am told, many people, especially in the USA, take this as an article of faith. I have never seen it in any of the old books of magic, and I think Gerald invented it.

While researching the Three-fold Law, I took the liberty of writing several early authors who had referenced it in their books. The few responses I received were always the same; they did not know where it came from but it was known, at least as oral tradition, when they entered the Craft. Using the dates of their initiations, I hoped to at least obtain a starting point for my research. In this case, since Raymond Buckland was the first to be initiated of those authors who took the time to respond, I had a start date of 1963. Buckland was initiated as a Gardnerian by Lady Olwen, Gerald Gardner's last high priestess, before Gardner's death in 1964. Although Buckland recalled that Lady Olwen's coven referred to the three-fold law, he did not recall any mention of it by Gardner himself in their correspondences. I also knew from Margot Adler that it was known in the US at least orally, when she entered the Craft in 1972. "I know it was talked about the minute I entered the craft in the Brooklyn Pagan Way, and that was 1972, but whether it came in written or oral form, I don't know."[1] The Brooklyn Pagan Way was run by the New York Coven of Welsh Traditional Witches so the Law of Return had already disseminated outside of Gardnerian practice by 1972.

Starting with books published in the 1960s, I sought to find any reference to the Three-fold Law or variations of that theme. I was particularly interested in finding non-Gardnerian sources since, unlike many other aspects of modern Wicca, the Three-fold Law appears to be a purely Wiccan construct particularly of Gardnerian lineage, adding a moral element to the practice of magic. I then worked backward seeking earlier influences, as well as forward, seeing who referenced these early books in their bibliographies.

Setting the Stage

At this point it may be useful to mention the types of witchcraft that existed, quite distinctly, in the 1960s and 1970s. It was only in the last two or three decades that Wicca became a melting pot of various influences and exploded into a plethora of traditions and viewpoints. I find the simplest breakdown was made in the book *Witches U.S.A.*, published in 1971 by Susan Roberts (a non-witch). I am elaborating on her descriptions, however, to better emphasize the distinctions. Solitary practice could fit under any of the below, except perhaps Gardnerian, since that was (and still is) essentially coven-centric.

- Ceremonial – Described in Roberts' book as practitioners of ceremonial magic, but really would include all practitioners of folk magic or natural magic, who work under or associate with the term "witch" but do not work with the religious aspects. I would probably just labeled this type as "non-religious witchcraft" since ceremonial magic was only one form of magic that may have been

---

[1] Alder, personal comment.

adopted, and probably not as widespread in witchcraft as the use folk magic, simple spells, divination, and herbalism. This would be the "witch" but not "Wiccan" category.

- Traditional – Various forms of (mostly) religious witchcraft based on various backgrounds and cultures (Celtic, Sicilian, Germanic, etc) depending on the group. Whether these traditions truly existed before Gardner went public or developed independently after being inspired by his ideas is debatable, since very few witches outside of the Gardnerian/Alexandrian line were public in the early 1970s.

- Hereditary – Basically Traditions that were handed down along family ties thus being more culturally specific. Some were more religion-oriented than others. This can get confusing because some hereditary traditions were later passed on outside a family lineage and thus could be considered an aspect of Traditional witchcraft previously described. Many feel that all traditional forms of Witchcraft were initially hereditary. Since it had become a trend to falsely claim to have been initiated by a member of one's family, as Alex Sanders became infamous for, the actual extent of hereditary witches is still questionable today.

- Gardnerian – The Gardnerian tradition (and offshoots like the Alexandrian tradition) were listed separately because of certain very distinctive elements. Gardnerians were almost unique in their insistence on working skyclad (nude), use of the scourge as a tool of the craft, and later because of their emphasis on ethics. Gardnerians also made much use of dance and chant to bring about ecstatic states. Hans Holzer, another early author, made the distinction that Gardnerians were more emotionally-oriented in their practice while non-Gardnerian based forms were more intellectually-oriented in their practice.[1]

Of the forms of witchcraft, those of Gardnerian lineage (including Alexandrians) were most pronounced in the press, particularly for their ritual nudity which had captured the public's attention. Today, we may be more apt to simply include the Gardnerian lineage under the general "traditional" category. But it is important to note that the generic Wicca of today is essentially a derivative of Gardnerian influence and practice that has evolved through the years to encompass various other influences including other forms of traditional witchcraft, Native American spirituality, and Voodoo.[2] This in itself would make an interesting topic for a paper and will be addressed at another time. The point now is to underline the influence the Gardnerian lineage has had on the development of Wicca.

Most of the early authors involved in Witchcraft, such as Gardner, Sanders, Valiente, Buckland, the Farrars, and the Crowthers, were either Gardnerian or Alexandrian and so these traditions have had the greatest influence on the growing number of people seeking information on the Craft. Even Dr. Leo Louis Martello, who started out as Strega, was initiated into both the Gardnerian and Alexandrian traditions around 1969 as his books on witchcraft began to be published.

Note that when the Alexandrian Tradition was formed by Alex Sanders in the mid-to-late 1960s, it was presented as a completely separate (but similar) tradition from the Gardnerians. It was not until later that it was discovered that Alex had obtained a copy of a Gardnerian book of shadows which he passed off as his own. Stewart and Janet Farrar later separated themselves from Alex, whose behavior and extravagant claims had become

---

[1] Hans Holzer, *The Truth about Witchcraft,* 1971, page 134.

[2] In the United States the use of shaped candles and oils and powders like "separation" and "hexing" were labeled "voodoo" or "hoodoo" until witches began to incorporate these practices into their own.

questionable, and continued to evolve the Alexandrian tradition as a distinct but related tradition from the Gardnerians. I am therefore presenting them as a branch on the Gardnerian line of witchcraft in this chapter.

Gardnerians were often accused (sometimes justly) of implying that they were the only real form of witchcraft. Part of the reason for this was that prior to Gerald Gardner, the idea of a modern practice of witchcraft was simply not known to the public. In fact, even now it is still hard to prove without doubt that they *did* exist before Gardner. What is known as the Feri tradition (from Cora and Victor Anderson) today is one of the few examples with early roots, but even that began adapting publicly available Gardnerian and Alexandrian material in the 1970s. One could justly argue it evolved to a form of Wicca at that time. However, Gardner said he wrote his books in the 1950s and 1960s in hopes of saving what he thought was a religion on the verge of fading away. Since this was at a time when modern witchcraft was unknown, this indeed seemed to be the case. This thinking is why Buckland wrote in a small handbook called *Witchcraft – The Religion* in 1966:

> In only recent years did the Craft come to America. This is understandable when it considered that the time that this country was first being populated was in the time of the fierce prosecutions of the witches in Europe. One or two individual witches may have come here but it is doubtful if complete covens did. The individual witch family in all probability died out, so there is no long background of true witchcraft in the United States.[1]

This statement was probably not intended as an implication against non-Gardnerian forms of witchcraft, but rather a simple observation of the apparent state of witchcraft at the time. The few known early covens in the United States had been founded primarily by Raymond Buckland and Lady Rowan, his wife at

---

[1] Buckland, Raymond, *Witchcraft – The Religion* (pamphlet), 1966, page 13.

the time, and were thus Gardnerian. Buckland later established other traditions (Seax-Wica and Pecti-Wita), which still carried a similar format as the Gardnerians (albeit less rigid and more welcoming to solitary practice) and with ethics when it came to karma and the three-fold law.

The reason for the short history lesson is to set the stage for the environment of witchcraft in its various forms as it began to merge and homogenize in the 1970s into the modern forms of Wicca. Although some traditions, such as Gardnerian, remain relatively intact today, it is now a minority to newer forms that in some way have been influenced by the Gardnerian tradition or one of its offshoots. The Wicca of today is in many ways not the witchcraft of twenty years ago, but evidence of the influence of Gardner and his line of witchcraft lies just under the surface of many modern Wiccan beliefs – even that of such radical traditions as the Dianic Tradition.

Rise of the Three-Fold Law

An early hint of the three-fold law can be found in Gerald Gardner's book *High Magic's Aid* (1949). Fearing the public's reaction to a book on witchcraft, Gardner used the pen name Scire (his craft name), and presented his information, including parts of actual Gardnerian initiation rituals, in the form of a work of fiction. It was with this book that Gardner gauged the interest and sincerity of his potential students.

During the second-degree initiation into "the brotherhood," as the Craft was referred to in the book, the initiate returns the number of scourges received three-fold onto the one doing the initiating (as is done in the actual Gardnerian and Alexandrian rituals). The author then comments: "For this is the joke in witchcraft, the witch knows, though the initiate does not, that she will get three times what she gave, so she does not strike hard."[1]

Since I could find no elaboration on the meaning behind this comment from the later writings of Gardner I cannot assume with confidence that *his* intention behind this ritual return of the scourging onto the initiator was implicitly a moral statement or whether it was symbolic that that initiated was now on equal grounds with the initiator. (Or arguably that he was just into scourging, which many believe he did enjoy.[2])

Stewart Farrar did link this portion of the initiation with the Three-fold Law, and his work was not only instrumental in the fine-tuning of the Alexandrian tradition, but also served as a basis for many other forms of Wicca that derived from Gardnerian/Alexandrian roots.

> "...the ritual using of the cords and the scourge is the occasion for dramatizing a lesson about what is often called 'the boomerang effect'; namely, that any magical effort, whether beneficent or malicious, is liable to rebound threefold on the person who makes it."[3]

However, even those who worked closely with Gardner, such as Doreen Valiente, could offer no definitive answer to Gardner's personal take on the Three-fold Law. In an interview in 1991, Valiente states, "I think old Gerald cooked it up in one of his rituals, and people took it terribly literally."[4]

Valiente was an early initiate and high priestess of Gardner, being initiated by him in 1953. She is sometimes referred to as the "Mother of Witchcraft" because of her extensive collaboration with Gardner in reworking his notes into a more formal book of

---

[1] Scire (Gardner, Gerald), *High Magic's Aid*, 1996, page 188.
[2] This idea is discussed in depth in Aidan Kelly's *Crafting the Art of Magic: Book 1*, (Llewellyn, 1991).
[3] Farrar, Janet and Stewart, *A Witches Bible Compleat*, 1984, page 24.
[4] Doreen Valiente, 1991 Interview with FireHeart Journal.

shadows. One of her more most well-known contributions is the poetic form of the Charge of the Goddess.

That the Three-fold Law became an aspect of the Gardnerian Tradition is not at doubt. The concept was not only taught by Buckland as he founded Gardnerian covens throughout the United States, but Buckland can trace this teaching to Lady Olwen[1] (Monique Wilson), a high priestess who was initiated by Gerald Gardner himself.

> The threefold law was very definitely a part of what I was taught by Lady Olwen (who was, of course, taught by Gerald). Now to be honest I cannot remember if the term "three fold LAW" was used but definitely "the law of threefold return" was used. But they amount to the same, of course.[2]

Although Lady Olwen taught what amounted to the Three-fold Law, Gardner never made such a reference in his correspondences with Buckland. Buckland had been corresponding with Gardner even before his initiation, and was only later initiated by Lady Olwen in 1963 after finally meeting Gardner in person. (In the Gardnerian tradition, one is always initiated by a member of the opposite sex, so Gardner could not initiate Buckland himself.)

Since Gardner believed in karma, and karma is often confused with or considered the force behind, the three-fold law, it is my opinion (since I lack direct evidence) that while Gardner probably made common reference to karma to his students in conversation, the three-fold law was often *inferred* by initiates (both Gardnerian and Alexandrian) during their second-degree initiations as a

---

[1] It is difficult to gain much non-biased information on Lady Olwen. After Gardner's death in 1964 she inherited his witchcraft museum on the Isle of Man, and upset many witches by selling the museum, along with Gardner's notebooks, to Ripley's International. I have heard numerous times through word of mouth that she had a propensity for passing off her own opinions as Gardnerian teachings, but I have never heard this from anyone with first-hand experience.

[2] Private correspondence with Raymond Buckland in 2000.

literal law and manifestation of karma. Those who did not take the literal meaning too seriously used variations such as the Law of Return or the Boomerang effect, which could more easily fit into a general occult context.

> Belief in the simple law of cause and effect is a popular one among witches of all traditions; however, this particular way of expressing it [the three-fold law] seems to have originated with the Gardnerians and is peculiar to their English tradition.[1]

Gardnerians who did not work with Lady Olwen or Raymond Buckland did not have this emphasis on a three-fold return. Arnold and Patricia Crowther, for example, who were initiated in 1960 (Patricia by Gardner and Arnold by Patricia), make very little reference to ethics at all in their initial books published in the 1970s[2], although they did believe in a form of return. "Witches believe in a kind of Karma, that evil returns on the evil-doer."[3]

Valiente, who was initiated by Gardner in 1953 and rewrote much of Gardner's early book of shadows, never mentions the Three-fold law in her early work and even went so far as to question its validity in a 1991 interview – a time when the Three-fold Law was a common belief.

> Personally, I've always been skeptical about it because it doesn't seem to me to make sense. I don't see why there has to be one special law of karma for Witches and a different one for everybody else. I don't buy that.[4]

Unlike the Crowthers however, Valiente, along with several other coven members, split from Gardner around 1960 due to his habit of presenting his personal opinions as law. Valiente then

---

[1] Roberts, Susan, *Witches U.S.A.*, 1971.
[2] Patricia Crowther did reference it in 1981 in her book *Lid of the Cauldron*, but by then the Three-Fold Law had already been in circulation.
[3] Crowther, Arnold and Patricia, *The Secrets of Ancient Witchcraft*, 1974.
[4] Doreen Valiente, 1991 Interview with FireHeart Journal.

continued her studies in the Craft by researching Gardner's sources and seeking other traditional forms of witchcraft.

Law of Return and Karma

It is worth pointing out that although reincarnation is generally considered a core belief in modern Wicca, very little emphasis is typically placed on the process itself, and many Wiccans and pagans have a tendency to believe that we work out this "karmic debt" (for lack of a better term) in the *present life*.

In Hinduism, which is where the concept of karma originates, karma is an aspect of reincarnation and influences the environment of our future lives. However, since some witches do not believe our actions influence future lives, sometimes karma in Wicca is associated with the cause and effect principle within the present life only. This process is sometimes presented as "retribution" in order to avoid confusion with the Hindu context of karma, but "retribution" can infer an outside intelligent agent behind the process, causing further misunderstanding of its own.

A good early example of this can be found in Buckland's *Witchcraft from the Inside*, first published in 1971:

> It is a belief that each incarnation will be better than the previous one; there is only progression, no regression. Along with this belief goes another – in retribution in the present life. It is thought that whatever is done returns three-fold. If good is done then good will return threefold in the same life; but if evil is done, then that too will return threefold *in this life*. [Italics as presented in the text][1]

Since Buckland did not believe that this "retribution" carried over, he did not use the term "karma" to describe it. However, not all authors shared this view and some, such as the Farrars,

---

[1] Buckland, Raymond, *Witchcraft from the Inside*, 1971, page 69.

stressed karma as an aspect of reincarnation, where our future lives are dependant upon how we live our present life.

Typically, the more emphasis on the three-fold law, the less emphasis on karma, but these variations among authors would attribute for much of the confusion today where karma – an already misunderstood concept in the West – is used synonymously with the Law of Return, or as the Law of Return as it manifests in future lives.

Law of Return as Divine Justice

Although not usually taken to the point of literal divine justice, it is quite common today for witches seeking justice when wronged to take comfort in the Law of Return, knowing that those who wronged them will eventually "get what they deserve." This is quite similar to Christians who take comfort in knowing that anyone who seems to get away with an injustice now will *eventually* pay for it, if not in this life, then at their final judgment by God. This "fail safe" mechanism is carried over in the westernized concept of karma shared by many Wiccans where one's future life is the manifestation of the working out of unpaid "karmic debt."

A very interesting association of the Law of Return as the working of the Greek goddess Nemesis, a form of Divine Justice, can be found in Justine Glass' book, *Witchcraft, The Sixth Sense* published in 1965. "The witches see eventualities of this kind as the outworking of Nemesis, or the law of come-back."[1]

In my book, *Out of the Shadows: An Exploration of Dark Paganism and Magick*, I briefly discuss Nemesis:

> Nemesis: (Greek) Goddess of divine anger and daughter of
> Night (the goddess Nyx), Nemesis is the instrument through

---

[1] Glass, Justine, *Witchcraft, The Sixth Sense*, 1965, page 135.

which the gods punished those who grew too proud through wealth and fame, or who angered the gods. Her vengeance is inflexible and inescapable. As time went on, Nemesis gradually was softened into a kinder goddess of destiny, known as Adrasteia, "The Inevitable One", whom no one could escape. Adrasteia would bring sickness to those who abused their body and destruction to those parts of the earth we did not treat appropriately. Nemesis is also the goddess of law and retribution, often portrayed as a winged woman carrying a sword or whip and riding through the air on a chariot drawn by griffins.[1]

I have only seen one other association of the Three-fold law with Nemesis, and that was around 1973 when Dr. Leo Louis Martello first published his book *Witchcraft: The Old Religion*. In that book, he explains why he had chosen the Craft name "Nemesis."

> I chose it [the craft name Nemesis] because it's the name of the Greek Goddess of retributive justice. All Witches claim to believe in Karma, and one of their tenets is "Do good and it will return to you threefold. Do evil and it will return to you threefold."[2]

In the case of Justine Glass, I am not sure if this association with Nemesis was her interpretation, or something that she had read elsewhere. Sadly, her book rarely specified sources and was often worded in a way that made her knowledge of the Craft questionable. For example, her use of the phrase "law of come-back" was not a common descriptive for the concept and may have been due to unintentional paraphrasing as an outsider who would not be familiar with the colloquialism of the Craft.

Doreen Valiente also mentions that Robert Cochrane had misled[3] Glass while consulting her in the writing of her book. "Cochrane

---

[1] Coughlin, John J., *Out of the Shadows: An Exploration of Dark Paganism and Magick*, 2000, page 162.

[2] Martello, Dr. Leo Louis, *Witchcraft: The Old Religion*, 1973, page 270.

[3] It should be noted that in the early 1970s many authors who were not witches began to publish books on their experiences with witches during their research process. Also many publishers, wanting to cash in on this growing interest in the occult, were quick to encourage their authors to do so. These authors did not always understand the nuances of

pulled poor Justine Glass's leg unmercifully and shamelessly admitted to me that he had done so."[1]

Outside of Witchcraft, H. P. Blatavasky related some aspects of Karma to Nemesis in the late 19th century, but Blatavasky's influence in Wiccan thought is more indirect, being through the works of later occultists such as Dion Fortune. Blatavasky and her work in theosophy were significant for bringing eastern thought (including concepts such as karma and reincarnation) to the West and attempting to present it in a way that western culture could understand.

In *Aradia: The Gospel of the Witches*, a book that was first published in 1899 and was of significant influence to Gerald Gardner and other early authors, a particular verse stands out as a possible relative to the Law of Return:

> And when a priest shall do you injury
> By his benedictions, ye shall do to him
> Double the harm, and do it in the name
> Of me, *Diana*, Queen of witches all.[2]

Although not very Wiccan sounding, this can be taken in a similar context with the working of Nemesis – both being forms of divine justice. In the case of the above quote from *Aradia*, however, the return is greater than the initial action, much like the three-fold law, but the retribution is done in the name of Diana instead of by the Goddess directly.

Patricia Crowther also connects the Three-fold Law as possibly being a form of divine justice in 1981:

---

the practice nor could they always clearly delineate the various "types" of witches (such as Gardnerian as apposed to hereditary witches) from each other. It was also quite easy for such uninitiated authors to be mislead by the personal agendas and egos of those they interviewed, not to mention for the author and/or publisher to only include that information which best fit what they wanted or expected.

[1] Valiente, Doreen, *The Rebirth of Witchcraft*, 1989, page 121.

[2] Leland, Charles, *Aradia: The Gospel of the Witches*, 1968, page 5.

> "...if a witch *did* intentionally set out to harm anyone, he (or she) would not only be breaking a very strict law, thus incurring the wrath of the Goddess, but would also be putting himself (or herself) in jeopardy, as the magic performed would rebound on them three-fold."[1]

Although I have not seen it specifically referenced in books on witchcraft, Dion Fortune's belief in "The Watchers" as psychic police is worth exploration since, as it will be noted in the next section, her work has been extremely influential in the development of modern Wicca, not to mention other aspects of the occult.

> ...the watchers, that curious section of the occult hierarchy which is concerned with the welfare of nations. A certain section of their work is apparently concerned with the policing of the astral plane. Very little is actually known about them.... [some text skipped]... whenever black magic is afoot, they set to work to put a spoke in its wheels.[2]

Fortune was not sure if these Watchers were still human (physical beings) or if they existed only on the astral plane, but she sensed their workings and influence on several occasions against those who worked black magic. (Fortune had a penchant for portraying this sense of an ongoing battle as also being waged secretly between black lodges and white lodges. In fact, just as there was much overlap of her occult studies into her fictional novels, one can argue the reverse as well.)

In *The Witches Way* (published in 1981) and later *A Witches Bible Compleat*[3] (1984), the Farrars make an interesting point to the question of how a witch, adhering to the maxim of "harm none," can avoid the fate of being taken advantage of by the less scrupulous. Interestingly, the response (the use of a binding spell) not only eloquently portrays the witch's stance of protection

---

[1] Crowther, Patricia, *Lid off the Cauldron*, 1981, page 6.

[2] Fortune, Dion, *Psychic Self-Defense*, 1999, page 155.

[3] *A Witches Bible Compleat* contains the full text of both *Eight Sabbats for Witches* and *The Witches' Way*.

without harm but also hints at an external equalizing force associated with Karma.

> The very specific purpose of a binding spell is to render the evil actions powerless – not to harm or punish the wrongdoer; punishment can be safely left to the Lords of Karma.[1]

The reference of "Lords of Karma" is not common in witchcraft, although it can found in the works of Dion Fortune. The idea of an external *intelligent* agent was the Farrars' way of incorporating general occult theory, such as Dion Fortune's concept of the Watchers and the Lords of Karma, into a more Wiccan context. As will be seen in the next section, Stewart Farrar often sought to associate general occult theory with Wiccan beliefs.[2]

> We have spoken of karma as an almost impersonal process, set in train by the inexplicable laws of cause and effect. And that *is* its basic principle in action. But that does not mean there is no intervention or that what are sometimes called 'the Lords of Karma' are mere observers. Higher entities of many kinds do exist and function on the non-material planes, intermediate between humankind and the ultimate creative force as every religion.[3]

Law of Return as Occult Principle

The initial books on witchcraft were primarily geared towards dispelling some of the myths about witches and concentrated on history and some of the basic beliefs of the Craft. As authors began to delve deeper into the practice itself, many took the liberty of elaborating on the details of their beliefs. Sadly, the few

---

[1] Farrar, Janet and Stewart, *A Witches Bible Compleat*, 1984, volume 2, page 141.
[2] Upon re-reading Stewart Farrar's books after recently researching Dion Fortune's works, it would not be an exaggeration to state that Stewart's version of Witchcraft was based on the Gardnerian Book of Shadows and filled in with the work of Dion Fortune. Fortune was clearly a significant influence in Stewart's beliefs and her work is reflected in Stewart's writings more than any other Wiccan author.
[3] Farrar, Janet and Stewart, *A Witches Bible Compleat*, 1984, volume 2, page 123.

books that mentioned the Three-fold Law, or one of its variations, did little more than claim that it was something to which witches abided.

Between 1969 and 1971 many accounts of modern witchcraft by non-witches (or novice or heavily-closeted witches) began to be published. Although they did not include much useful information of the Craft, they did generate interest – and a market – that cried out for more details.

One author to respond to this call was Stewart Farrar, who was later initiated and became a very prominent figure in the Craft. In 1971, his book *What Witches Do* gave an inside view of Craft practice and beliefs. Farrar also made an interesting reference to the workings of the three-fold law in magic.

> "The 'white' witch, however, maintains that 'black' working, while it may be initially successful, carries the seeds of its own retribution. Not only does power misused corrupt the user; it can also have a boomerang effect. It is a well-established occult principle that psychic attack which comes up against a stronger defense rebounds threefold upon the attacker. Like the hi-fi amplifier again, feed-back can build into a scream of self-torment which overloads the whole circuit."[1]

Stewart then went on to offer a quote from Dion Fortune to supply a metaphysical explanation for the boomerang effect of "black" working. Forune portrays the soul "moving with the tide of evolution"[2] like a wheel spinning clockwise and a soul moving against that tide as a wheel spinning counter-clockwise. The normal flow would be clockwise, but "black" workings would reverse that spin. The warning comes as a reminder of momentum: a wheel spinning counterclockwise cannot just

---

[1] Farrar, Stewart, *What Witches Do*, 1991, page 37.
[2] Fortune, Dion, *Psychic Self-Defense*, 1999, page 135.

reverse its direction. "Momentum has to be checked and worked up again before reversal of spin can take place."[1]

The reference to Dion Fortune above is actually very important here because it clearly shows her influence on the development of modern Wiccan concepts. Like Stewart, Gerald Gardner was well read in Dion Fortune's books and includes several of them in his bibliographies. In fact, after reading many of the works of Dion Fortune, one can better understand Gardner's emphasis on polarity, gender, and the sexual elements of Wiccan symbolism, not to mention much of the anti left-hand path sentimentality, particularly prevalent in Stewart Farrar's books. Look in the bibliography of many of the early authors, such as Gardner, Valiente, the Farrars, and Martello, and you will find books by Dion Fortune listed – often several of them.

Getting back to the Three-fold law and its birthing place in occult principles, I offer the following quote from Dion Fortune's book, *Psychic Self-Defense*, first published in 1930:

> "It is a well-known cosmic law that everything moves in circles, and whatever forces we send out, and whatever thought-forms we extrude from our auras, unless absorbed by the object to which they are directed, will return to us in due course. One of the most effective, and also one of the most widely practiced methods of occult defense is to refuse to react to an attack, neither accepting nor neutralizing the forces projected against one, and thus turning them back on their sender. We must never overlook the fact that a so-called occult attack may be evil though-forms returning home to roost."[2]

The reference of the Three-fold Law as the "Law of Return" fits much better in this context, as does the metaphysical explanation offered by Dion Fortune. One of the reasons for the debate of the validity of the Three-fold Law is due to the law's often-moralistic

---

[1] Fortune, Dion, *Psychic Self-Defense*, 1999, page 136.

[2] Fortune, Dion, *Psychic Self-Defense*, 1999, pages 77-78.

presentation, which comes across more as a religious belief or ethical stance than a universal occult principle.

When taken out of its ethical context the idea of the Law of Return begins to become more palatable to non-Wiccan occultists. Although not all practitioners of magic would agree with Fortune's theory of the spin of the soul, very few would doubt that just as a child can get burned while playing with fire, so too can a practitioner get burned should one improperly handle the forces raised when working magic, regardless of the intention. The magician would also be reminded that what we think we need is not always what we really need and this too can often sow the seeds of our own destruction. It is only when the practice of magic is encompassed in religious practice does it begin to take on a moral context.

A similar approach was taken by another well-known public figure in modern Witchcraft, Sybil Leek. In 1971, she warned "...there is generally a kickback in black magic (many spells reverse themselves against the spell-maker)."[1]

Another occult principle that can account for the concept of the Law of Return is the Law of Attraction. This theory of "like attracts like" is the underlying principle of sympathetic magic and even the underlying logic behind the use of correspondences in magic. For example, in sympathetic magic, one would ritually act out the desired results in order to bring about those results; the classic example being how hunters in certain tribal cultures will enact a successful hunt in dance prior to the hunt. When using correspondences, one would use objects (herbs, stones, etc) and colors associated with the desired goal as a means of attracting similar energies. For example, in a love spell the colors red and pink might be used in conjunction with rose oil and rose quartz because all of these are associated with love.

---

[1] Leek, Sybil, *The Complete Art of Witchcraft*, 1971, page 76.

However, the Law of Attraction can also be used outside of a magical context. Simply put, the Law of Attraction states that the universe will respond similarly to where we put our energy, including thoughts and emotions. A drastic but universal example is when we have a "bad day" where things continually go wrong. During such a time, we tend to cling to a pessimistic attitude that expects – consciously or not – continued failure. It is often only when we are distracted long enough to take our minds (including unconscious) off our dilemma that things begin to return to status quo. The theory has become quite a fad today in certain self-help and productivity-enhancing seminars and is often abused. In fact a search for the "law of attraction" or "like attracts like" on the Internet is more likely to bring you to a website of a "coach" on this technique than on an occult-related subject.

For one to work harmful magic against someone, one must concentrate on such feelings as anger and hatred. In such a state, it can be argued, one becomes susceptible to those same forces, much as a speaker too close to a microphone is subject to feedback. Although this risk of feedback is not guaranteed, it can easily be presented as or mistaken for an ethical principle. In his introduction to the book *Applied Magic*, by Dion Fortune, Gareth Knight presents this concept in a particularly moralistic way, not unlike that of Dion Fortune, who also took a very moralistic approach to her work.

> In the esoteric sphere there is also the cosmic law "like attracts like" which, on the one hand, can lead the aspiring soul toward the heights through contact with inner guides and helpers, and on the other, attract degraded inner entities to drag the erring soul unto a negative spiral that can lead ultimately to self-destruction.[1]

A similar occult law was presented as the "Law of Action and Reaction" in the book *A Compendium of Occult Laws* by R.

---

[1] Fortune, Dion, *Applied Magic*, 2000, page xiii.

Swinburne Clymer which was in publication at least as far back as 1938. Clymer (1878-1966) was an influential and high-ranking Rosicrucian who founded The Rosicrucian Brotherhood in Quakertown, Pennsylvania in 1902.

> Whatever man does or desires will always produce a corresponding reaction both upon himself and all things with which he is allied or connected. He who benefits others in dire need is actually helping himself, while he who works injury to another, though ever so slightly, is decreeing his own punishment. The acts of men are the external manifestation of their own interior existence, and every thought and act as a natural tendency to repeat itself.[1]

Even earlier occult principles such as Magnetism provides an occult principle that can be related in an ethical context to that of the Law of Return. Eliphas Lévi (1810-1875) stated that the "magnetism of those who are good attracts to them all that is good for them"[2] just as those who are evil will attract the opposite. The reason for this being that "positive magnetism is a force which gathers things together, whereas negative magnetism is a dispersive force. Light attracts life and fire carries destruction with it."[3]

In other words, for one to work harm on another one must "polarize" oneself to the negative, where those destructive forces can be harnessed, and in so doing one opens oneself to that same energy. Of course it must be noted that his work, despite its significant influence and importance in occultism, were often plagued with contradictions as he sought a balance between his occult philosophy and his devotion to the Catholic Church. (Don't underestimate Lévi's indirect significance to Wicca; The concepts of invoking and banishing pentagrams, as well as the negative connotation of the inversed pentagram, were all derived from the work of Lévi.)

---

[1] Clymer, R. Swinburne, *A Compendium of Occult Laws*, 1966, page 115.
[2] Lévi, Eliphas, *The Great Secret or Occultism Unveiled*, 2000, page 185.
[3] Lévi, Eliphas, *The Great Secret or Occultism Unveiled*, 2000, page 185.

Why Three-Fold?

Although we have seen some of the logic for the development of the Law of Return as a core belief in modern Wicca, where did the Law of Return as a *three-fold* return come into being?

Despite much of the Gardnerian Book of Shadows remaining secret to this day, I was able to locate an interesting passage in the second degree initiation in the Public contents of the Gardnerian Book of Shadows. (The initiation rituals are circa 1949.)

> Magus: "Thou hast obeyed the Law. But mark well, when thou receivest good, so equally art bound to return good threefold."[1]

Three is a very significant number in this public Gardnerian material, much of which is also found in the Farrars' *A Witches Bible Compleat* and appears frequently in their rituals, particularly during initiation.

- There are three degrees of initiation.

- The Gardnerian magic circle consists of three circles, an inner circle surrounded by two outer circles.

- Magus closes a doorway that was opened in a circle by drawing the point of the sword across the opening three times, joining all three circles, saying, "Agla, Azoth, Adonai," followed by drawing three pentacles to seal it.

- The circle is often circumambulated three times during ritual.

---

[1] Kelly, Aidan , Public contents of the Gardnerian Book of Shadows (sacred-texts.com), "The Initiation (1949)," see Second Degree or Kelly, Aidan, *Crafting the Art of Magic: Book 1*, 1991, page 59.

- When the magus rings the bell in ritual it is rung three times.

- Five is said to be a fortunate number because "three added to two (the Perfect Couple) be five."

- In second degree the initiate returns the number of strokes of the scourge three-fold onto the initiator.

It is easy to see that the three-fold law could easily be inferred by an initiate, particularly during the second degree initiation, and that if one would receive good three times then so would it be with the inverse, and so bad deeds would result in a three-fold penalty. Whether this was actually taught by Gardner or simply inferred by his students is still debatable. Even Valiente, one of Gardner's original high priestesses, did not claim out-right that Gardner created the Three-fold Law. Going back to my email from Raymond Buckland, who was one of the first authors to publish the Three-fold Law in a book, Buckland learned it as the oral tradition of his coven and not directly from Gardner.

As is even seen today, prominent authors and community leaders can be easily taken literally, and so Gardner's symbolic used of the number three may have been taken literally by those who followed him. Since early Gardnerians did not make mention of the Three-fold Law, it is in my opinion that it was a latter edition that began though Lady Olwen's interpretation of Gardner's work, and carried on through Buckland into the United States where it gained popularity, primarily though his significant visibility in the press and his books.

As other traditions began to develop and solitary practice began to surpass coven practice, the Three-fold Law offered a useful way to keep those dabbling in magic in check. Covens were portrayed by Gardner and others as functioning as a balancing agent in keeping us from abusing magic or acting foolishly. As solitary practice gained momentum, this failsafe was left to catch phrases such as the Rede and the Three-fold Law. While the Rede neatly summarized the principle of "harm none" the Three-fold Law added the "or else!" which western culture has a tendency to emphasize.

Timeline for Some Law of Return Concepts

Date (1st Published)	Title/Author	Tradition of Author	Phrase
1930	*Psychic Self-Defense,* Dion Fortune	Not involved in witchcraft but influenced many early Wiccans.	"It is a well-known cosmic law that everything moves in circles, and whatever forces we send out, and whatever thought-forms we extrude from our auras, unless absorbed by the object to which they are directed, will return to us in due course."
1949	*High Magic's Aid,* Scire (Gerald Gardner)	Gardnerian	"Thou hast obeyed the Law. But mark well, when thou receivest good, so equally art bound to return good threefold. (For this is the joke in witchcraft, the witch knows, though the initiate does not, that she will get three times what she gave, so she does not strike hard.)"

1965	*Witchcraft, The Sixth Sense,* Justine Glass	Outsider (at that time at least)	"The witches see eventualities of this kind as the outworking of Nemesis, or the law of come-back"
1968	*Beyond* magazine, October 1968, article by Raymond Buckland "I Live with a Witch"[1]	Gardnerian (Buckland, not the magazine)	Ray Buckland: "Another of our beliefs is in retribution *in this life.* We believe that whatever we do will return threefold in this life. Do good to someone and you will receive three times as much good in return. But do evil, and that, too, will return triple."

---

[1] It should be noted that Mr. Buckland had appeared in many articles and TV shows earlier than the 1968 issue of *Beyond.* I am still attempting to locate these and find earlier references to the Three-fold Law. I have yet to find mention of the Three-fold Law in print prior to Gardner's death in 1964. Thus far I did locate another 1968 article clipped from a newspaper called the *Sunday News* which also mentions "they believe that what a human being does in his life will return to him threefold."

1970	*Ancient and Modern Witchcraft,* Raymond Buckland	Gardnerian	"There is no need for a Hell, or Final Judgment, in witchcraft because of their belief in retribution in the present life. It is thought that whatever you do will return three-fold. If you do good then you will receive three times as much good. If you do evil, then that too will return at three times the strength." (p. 141)
1970	*Modern Witchcraft,* Frank Smyth	Outsider	"Witches believe that any act of magic rebounds thricefold on the operator."
1971	*Witchcraft from the Inside,* Raymond Buckland	Gardnerian	"It is thought that whatever is done returns three-fold. If good is done then good will return threefold in the same life; but if evil is done, then that too will return threefold *in this life.*"

1971	*Witches U.S.A.,* Susan Roberts	Outsider, but this quote references Gardnerian beliefs	Quotes an article from Buckland in the October 1968 issue of *Beyond*. Roberts also goes on to say ,"Belief in the simple law of cause and effect is a popular one among witches of all traditions; however, this particular way of expressing it seems to have originated with the Gardnerians and is peculiar to this English tradition." (p. 131)
1971	*What Witches Do,* Stewart Farrar	Alexandrian	"It is a well-established occult principle that psychic attack which comes up against a stronger defense rebounds threefold upon the attacker."
1971	*The Complete Art of Witchcraft,* Sybil Leek	"Hereditary" yet later found she worked upon a very Gardnerian-like foundation.	"...There is generally a kickback in black magic (many spells reverse themselves against the spell-maker)..." (p. 76)

1971	*The Wiccan,* March 1971, Number 19	(No context given)	Letter regarding Dr. Leo Louis Martello's comments of fighting back as self-defense: "We think such a situation can be amply dealt with by the Lords of Karma."
1972	*The Witch's Bible,* Gavin and Yvonne Frost	Celtic Wicca, Church of Wicca (Very controversial as to whether they are "Wiccan" or another construct completely but their correspondence course and occasional quotes in books and newspapers carried their views to many.)	"Good begets good; evil begets evil. There is a reaction to all positive and negative thoughts and deeds." (p. 19)
1972	*Black Magic, Satanism, and Voodoo,* Dr. Leo Louis Martello	(This was a generalization.)	"…witches believe 'bad returns threefold'"
1972	*The Villanovan,* March 22, 1972 (quoting Dr. Leo Louis Martello)	(This was a generalization.)	"Do a good deed, it will return three-fold; do an evil deed, it will return three-fold."

1973	*The Witch's Workbook*, Ann Grammary	Author does not state but gives impression she is a witch or in the know. She pulls from many sources.	"The Law of Three: This is the term applied to a phenomenon believed to be true by many Witches." Author then notes it has to do with *unjust* curses. Later she provides a spell to invoke this law for retribution.
1973	*The Witchcraft Report*, Hans Holzer	No context given. Author was initiated into a few traditions around this time but does not mention that.	"…do not seek magical paths for unworthy purposes, or to hurt anyone; that which you send forth may come back a hundredfold."
1974	*The Secrets of Ancient Witchcraft*, Arnold and Patricia Crowther	Gardnerian	"Witches believe in a kind of Karma, that evil returns on the evil-doer"
1976	*Witchcraft: The Old Religion*, Dr. Leo Louis Martello	Strega and then Gardnerian	All Witches claim to believe in Karma, and one of their tenets is "Do good and it will return to you threefold. Do evil and it will return to your threefold."

	Maxine: The Witch Queen, Maxine Sanders (Quoting Alex during her initiation in 1964)	Alexandrian	"For when in witchcraft you must ever give as you receive, as triple…"
1979	*Drawing Down the Moon,* Margot Adler	Welsh Traditional and then Gardnerian	"Many believe in the 'threefold law': that whatever you do returns to you threefold. Some witches don't believe in the threefold law, but most believe that you get back what you give out." (p. 112)
1981	*A Witches Bible Compleat* (Vol 2) or *The Witches' Way*,[1] Janet and Stewart Farrar	Alexandrian	"'the boomerang effect'; namely, that any magical effort, whether beneficent or malicious, is liable to rebound threefold on the person who makes it."

Conclusion

The notion of cause and effect is generally accepted by witches of all forms, although it has been perceived in many different ways. The Farrar's kept to the same lines as Dion Fortune, considering negative return a risk when working magic to harm. Early Gardnerians made no reference to a law of return outside of

---

[1] These are one and the same; *A Witches Bible Compleat* contains the full text of both *Eight Sabbats for Witches* and *The Witches' Way*.

accepting Karma, which Doreen Valiente said, "Gerald Gardner...was a strong believer in reincarnation and the working-out of karma."[1] The first mention of a Three-fold Law in print which I have been able to locate comes from Raymond Buckland, although he has shared that he had learned it from Lady Olwen, and seems to have been inferred from Gardnerian initiation practices by some Gardnerians who took the symbolism in such rituals literally.

What we are left with is not a clean timeline of one instance of a Law of Return which has evolved over time, but rather several instances of the concept, each with a very specific context which has sometimes blended to cause confusion.

Buckland is the primary source of the popularity of the Three-fold Law, having actively promoted it in the United States since he was initiated into the Gardnerian Tradition in 1964. There are no records that I have been able to find to date of earlier Gardnerians using this concept. Monique Wilson, who initiated Buckland and who Buckland said taught this principle, did not write any books. Buckland applied this law to *all* actions and not just a principle in magic. Buckland did not believe in the notion of karma affecting future lives. Although his emphasis on the three-fold nature of return varied, it is clear that it was taken literally and presented as such in both his books and articles. It was quickly adapted by many other traditions which formed in response to growing interest in the Craft.

The Farrars are the primary source of the *Law of Return* which was particularly more of an occult principle in regards to the *potential* consequences of magic and linked this to some extent with Karma.

These two principles initially developed independently by their respective advocates (especially in the United States) and both

---

[1] Valiente, Doreen, *Witchcraft for Tomorrow*, 1978, page 39.

view points were merged into an uneasy yet largely unquestioned notion of retribution based both on both karma and the Three-fold Law.

But why did so many take it so literally? Keep in mind most of the authors were new to the Craft when they were initiated, and started writing soon after their initiation. It is interesting to compare the early works of Buckland, Stewart Farrar, and Leo Louis Martello to their later works. Buckland, for example, was extremely hostile to homosexuality[1] and non-Gardnerian forms of witchcraft, and Martello hoped his first book on witchcraft, *Weird Ways of Witchcraft*, would remain buried in obscurity.[2]

Much of Stewart Farrar's early work, for example, was basically a rehash of Alex Sander's words. As Stewart began to make the teachings his own, he "learned to sort out the undeniable wheat from the regrettable chaff."[3] It is easy for us to look upon authors as experts and accept their words without question.

Wicca in particular has been influenced greatly by authors and publishers. The lack of anything beyond the plethora of 101-style books on the market today can be blamed at least in part for the "insta-witch" mentality that is often the topic of complaint. Many Pagans have become embittered with certain publishers, for example, for promoting trendiness and fluff more than well-researched material. But it is unfair to single them out. Although these publishers have released a number of questionable books, almost any publisher is going to be concentrating on profit over integrity. Publishers need to sell books to stay in business and so are more likely to invest in books that appeal to the masses. While this does not entirely excuse the lack of integrity found with certain publishers, it is an unfortunate reality that publishers will release fluff until the public shows there is a market for more

---

[1] Buckland, Raymond, *Witchcraft: Ancient and Modern*, 1970, page 176.

[2] Martello, Dr. Leo Louis, *Witchcraft: The Old Religion*, 1975, page 255.

[3] Farrar, Janet and Stewart, *A Witches Bible Compleat*, 1984, volume 1, page 17.

detailed material. This situation is a two edged sword given the number of Pagans today who prefer to stick with the basics.

Authors like Buckland, already having incorporated the literal form of the Three-fold Law into their work, naturally sought ways to justify or explain such beliefs through speculative metaphysics rather than threaten the stability of their belief system. Each following generation of authors continued this trend, either attempting to justify their ethical stance or present it without further elaboration.

Anton LaVey (1930–1997), the infamous founder of the Church of Satan in the United States during the 1960s, has this to say about the Three-fold Law:

> "White witchcraft groups spout the theory that if you curse a person, it will 'return to you three-fold,' 'come home to roost,' or in some way 'boomerang back to the curser,'" he states. "This is yet another indication of the guilt-ridden philosophy which is held by these neo-pagan, pseudo-Christian groups. These people want to delve into witchcraft, but cannot divorce themselves from the stigma attached to it."[1]

While there has always been a certain level of antagonism between Satanists and Wiccans, this observation has some merit. Looking back to my own experiences in the Craft, whenever someone found out I was a "witch" I almost always had to answer these questions: *"Do you worship Satan?"* and *"Do you hex people?"*

Since the 1990s, Wicca has become much more known to the public and yet I am still occasionally asked these questions. In the early 1980s, when the public was still largely unaware of the Craft, such questions were almost guaranteed. Many of us used the word "Wicca" because it lacked the negative imagery associated with the word "witch." This sadly has changed as

---

[1] Roberts, Susan, *Witches U.S.A.*, 1971, page 221.

"Wicca" began to be used in television shows as a fancy way to refer to a witch, but it was a helpful way while it lasted to refer to our beliefs without an initial biased reaction.

In answering these questions, catch phrases such as the Rede and the Three-fold Law made it easier to get our point across quickly. Telling someone: *"No, we do not believe in Satan and believe that if we do wrong it comes back to us three times"* left little room for debate. The Three-fold Law provided an easy quote for articles in newspapers and magazines by publicly-known witches such as Raymond Buckland, providing a convenient way to promote a more positive image.

The downside of this, which LaVey's attack hits dead on, is that apart from those who called themselves witches for the shock effect, many actively sought to separate themselves from the bad press and stigmatism attached to witchcraft. Satanists were (and still are) often portrayed as the "bad guys" and Wiccans as the "good guys." I recall reading things such as *"Satanists are anti-witches"* or *"Satanists use the inverted pentagram because they are opposite to us (good) witches."*

I can only imagine the uphill battle early American witches such as Buckland had to face on a daily basis, at a time when the only sources of good press for witchcraft were their own statements. It should come as no surprise that Buckland, as one of the earliest public representatives in the United States, also was the one to push the Three-fold Law so vehemently and why it was so readily adopted by other witches.

In comparing witchcraft in the United Kingdom to that of the United States in the early 1980s, James Bennett noted:

> English witchcraft tends to be more spontaneous and less dogmatic than in USA. Although I can only compare the practices of the Gardnerian branch of the Craft, I feel that the strong personalities of the Bucklands, (and another woman on Long Island,) moulded the craft into a structured,

theologically dogmatic movement which is perhaps quite different from what Gardner had in mind.[1]

Over succeeding generations, especially in the United States, these short ethical statements have been given more and more emphasis without appropriate elaboration. The Rede and Three-fold Law on their own do not provide a complete ethical system and many new to the Craft assume that they do.

Bibliography

Publications Referenced in this chapter:

Adler, Margot. Drawing Down the Moon. New York: Penguin/Arkana, 1986.

Beyond Magazine October 1968.

Blavatsky, H. P. The Secret Doctrine, Volume 1. Illinois: Theosophical Publishing House, 1993.

Buckand, Raymond. Ancient and Modern Witchcraft. New York: HC Publishers, 1970.

Buckand, Raymond. Witchcraft – The Religion. New York: Buckland Museum of Witchcraft and Magick, 1966.

Buckland, Raymond. Witchcraft from the Inside. Minnesota: Llewellyn Publications, 1971.

Clymer, R. Swinburne. A Compendium of Occult Laws. Pennsylvania: Beverly Hall Corporation, 1966.

Coughlin, John. Out of the Shadows: An Exploration of Dark Paganism and Magick. Indiana: 1stBooks Library, 2001.

---

[1] Article entitled "Witchcraft in a Cross-cultural Perspective," by James Bennett in *Quest* number 51, September 1982.

Crowther, Patricia and Arnold. The Witches Speak. New York: Samuel Weiser, 1976.

Crowther, Arnold and Patricia. The Secrets of Ancient Witchcraft New York: University Books, 1974.

Crowther, Patricia. Lid off the Cauldron. Maine: Samuel Weiser, 1981.

Farrar, Stewart. What Witches Do. Washington: Phoenix Publishing, 1991.

Farrar, Janet & Stewart. A Witches Bible Compleat. New York: Magickal Childe, 1984.

Farrar, Janet & Stewart. Spells and How they Work. Washington: Phoenix Publishing, 1990.

Fields, Essie. "Witches' Liberation Advocate Dispells [sic] Popular Black Magic Myths." The Villanovan March 22, 1972.

Fortune, Dion. Psychic Self-Defense. Maine: Samuel Weiser, 1999.

Fortune, Dion. Applied Magic. Maine: Samuel Weiser, 2000.

Glass, Justine. Witchcraft, The Sixth Sense. London: Wilshire Books, 1965.

Guiley, Rosemary Ellen. The Encyclopedia of Witches & Witchcraft. New York: Checkmark Books, 1999.

Grammary, Ann. The Witch's Workbook. New York: Pocket Books, 1973.

Green, Marian (ed.). Quest No 15, September 1973.

Green, Marian (ed.). Quest No 51, September 1982.

Holzer, Hans. The Truth about Witchcraft. New York: Doubleday, 1971.

Holzer, Hans. The Witchcraft Report. New York: Ace, 1973.

Holzer, Hans. Wicca: The Way of the Witches. New York: Mannor Books, 1979.

Kelly, Aidan A. Crafting the Art of Magic, Book 1. Minnesota: Llewellyn Publications, 1991.

Leek, Sybil. The Complete Art of Witchcraft. New York: Signet, 1971.

Leland, Charles. Aradia: The Gospel of the Witches. New York: Buckland Museum, 1968.

Lévi, Eliphas. The Great Secret or Occultism Unveiled. Maine: Weiser Books, 2000.

Lévi, Eliphas. Trancendental Magic. Maine: Weiser Books, 1999.

Martello, Dr. Leo Louis. Black Magic, Satanism, and Voodoo. New York: HC Publishers, 1972.

Martello, Dr. Leo Louis. Witchcraft: The Old Religion. New Jersey: Citadel Press, 1975.

Roberts, Susan. Witchcraft U.S.A. New York: Dell Publishing, 1971.

Sanders, Maxine. Maxine: The Witch Queen. London: Star Books, 1976.

Scire (now known to be Gerald Gardner). High Magic's Aid. West Virginia: Godolphin House, 1996.

Smyth, Frank. Modern Witchcraft. Maryland: Harrow Books, 1973.

<u>Sunday News</u> October 27, 1968. [Sadly the clipping did not indicate the periodical's location although it seemed local to New York.]

Valiente, Doreen. <u>The Rebirth of Witchcraft</u>. Washington: Phoenix Publishing, 1989.

Valiente, Doreen. <u>Witchcraft for Tomorrow</u>. Washington: Phoenix Publishing, 1978.

Online Documents referenced in this chapter:[1]

Public Contents of the Gardnerian Book of Shadows: www.sacred-texts.com/pag/gbos

Doreen Valiente 1991 Interview with FireHeart: www.earthspirit.com/fireheart/fhdv1.html

Doreen Valiente 1997 speech at National Conference of the Pagan Federation: users.drak.net/Lilitu/valiente.htm

Maxine Sander's Profile: www.maxinesanders.co.uk

Private Correspondences referenced in this chapter:

Margo Adler, 2000

Raymond Buckland, 2000

---

[1] As of May 2007 some of these links no longer exist but the saved text can be viewed at www.waningmoon.com/ethics/sources.

A Plea to Pagan Authors and their Respective Publishers and Readers

Pagan authors are the single most influential force in the shaping of the modern Pagan spiritual movement. In watching the trends the subject matter of books have taken since the 1960s, when Paganism as a viable spiritual alternative gained momentum, one can clearly see just how evident this is.

Newcomers, often fearing public recognition as a "pagan" or lacking local groups for guidance, rely on publications for their first contact and have placed their trust and spiritual well being in the hands of the authors. It is our responsibility as authors to provide accurate information and clearly delineate well-documented research from personal opinions and elaboration. To fall prey to our desires for recognition and money and continue to write books lacking depth or accuracy is an affront to the Goddess and Her children.

I ask – no beg – that authors put aside their pride and consider the consequences of their books, keeping the following in mind:

- Pseudo-history or history as one feels it "should be" does not constitute fact.

- Magic and spells are a small aspect of modern Pagan spirituality and not a necessary practice.

- Credibility comes not from one's spiritual lineage or initiatory degree, but by making an example through one's Work.

- Compromising quality for the sake of profit, recognition, or book count is to sell out your own spiritual kin.

- There is nothing wrong with sharing personal insight and talents in offering new ways to practice when done openly and with integrity.

- There are enough "cookie cutter" books on the market today based on the standard marketing template of generic basics and filler spells and rituals. What we need is depth in content and encouragement to practice what one learns.

- One does not need to fabricate a new ancient tradition to get one's point across.

I encourage readers to write to authors and their publishers and share your satisfaction or dissatisfaction with their work, boycotting those who continue to prey upon us and warp our religion into a playground for their fantasies and greed.

Remember that authors are not infallible and the number of published books or claimed pedigrees does not make them (including me) authorities by default. Question anything that does not feel right and never accept what others tell you simply because it is in print. *Anyone* can publish a book today if they can convince the publisher it will sell, and sadly it is often the empty books of silly spells and catchy covers that entice our youth.

Publishers will continue to promote what they feel the public wants. As an international community with realized marketing potential, we can influence publishers like never before. We can demand for quality and depth and in time the weight of our voices will begin to influence those responsible for quality control.

Supplemental Material

~ Appendix A ~
Notes on Asking Permission

The idea that one must ask permission before working magic on someone's behalf, even if it is a healing, is a relatively new addition or interpretation of the Wiccan ethical stance. It is also an often debated element of Wiccan ethics.

The arguments for this idea vary. There is the questionable claim that the unexpected energy could harm or shock the subject, to interpretations of the Rede that dictate that doing something without the recipient's knowledge is equivalent to going against their will and thus is a form of "harm."

Sadly, with the rise of "instant-Wicca" and lack of organized or in-depth study, often personal opinions are interpreted as ultimate truisms and accepted without question or reasoning. The fact that when I question this belief I am met with hostility or vague reasoning has been of great concern to me, since such reactions indicate a blind faith that can ultimately lead to fundamentalism.

Since it is not the scope of this paper to offer my personal opinion or to justify or disprove this belief, I hope to find and document significant references in the hopes of finding a pattern or path of influence. It also offers a chance for us to reflect on our personal beliefs in a non-threatening way, so that we can deepen our understanding of why we believe what we do. My goal is not to rock the boat for the sake of entertainment or to change the reader's view. I do hope, however, that the reader will walk away with a stronger foundation in those beliefs that the reader has accepted as his or her own.

Although I have not yet formally researched this aspect of Wiccan ethics, I have naturally been keeping an eye out for any ethical references while researching the various topics in this book. I have therefore decided to share with you what I have found so far in hopes that readers may be able to help by directing me to books and articles that discuss this topic.

I have yet to find any references at all prior to the 1980s in Wiccan/Witchcraft sources. However, the notion of requiring permission before working magic on someone's behalf is not unique to Wicca. In 1930, Dion Fortune published a book called *Psychic Self-Defense*, where she stated:

> ...any attempt to dominate others, or in any way to manipulate their minds without their consent, is an unwarrantable intrusion upon their freewill and a crime against the integrity of the soul. How can we judge the intimate spiritual needs of another, especially if that other has not elected to confide in us? What right have we to invade his spiritual privacy and thrust our tampering fingers into the wheels of his innermost being? It is so common a practice to send the names of people to healing circles with a request that they should be concentrated upon, without taking the preliminary precaution of asking their permission, that I have heard it announced from the platform of a large Spiritualist public meeting that only those cases could be taken up which gave their written consent.

Dion Fortune was a Christian who belonged to an area of occultism which concentrated on psychism and work on the Astral Plane. However, her books were influential to many areas of the occult, including Wicca. Early authors such as Gerald Gardner and Stewart Farrar drew upon much of Fortune's work. Farrar in particular referenced Fortune extensively in his books, although I do not recall the specific issue of asking permission coming up.

As with other aspects of Wiccan ethics, many ideas circulate orally or via small newsletters and so may have circulated informally for some time before being put into a book. Tracking ideas and influences can therefore be extremely challenging.[1]

Still, in researching early books on Wicca I hope to locate the traces of their source as well as determine their context. Only with such a baseline can we begin to see how Wiccan ethics has changed and who influenced those changes. Such an understanding, I feel, is essential in comprehending Wicca as a living religion.

---

[1] If anyone is open to helping my research by donating or selling old pagan magazines/journals/newsletters please find my contact info at JohnCoughlin.com.

~ Appendix B ~
King Who???

I am indebted to Dr. David R. Jones for two public responses he made on my initial announcement of my Wiccan ethics project as well as to my early inquiries into King Pausole which I share below. (See the chapter entitled *The Wiccan Rede: A Historical Journey* to see how this literary character fits in with Wiccan ethics.)

Letter one:

```
From: David R. Jones
Subject: Re: The Wiccan Rede: A Historical
Journey (essay)
Newsgroups: alt.pagan, alt.magick,
alt.religion.wicca
Date: 2001-08-06

Do what thou wilt shall be the law.

A few more details regarding King Pausole. I
have the French original [1], which has:

Code de Tryphême

I.        - Ne nuis pas à voisin.
```

II.   - Ceci bien compris, fais ce qu'il te plaît. (p. 14)

and the Lumley translation [2]. Now Lumley (p. 16) translates this into

Code of Tryphemiz

I.   Thou shalt not harm thy neighbor
II.   This being understood, do as you wouldst.

Now my poor French agrees with the first point, but the "wouldst" of point II. seems fairly weak for "plaît." which should be more like what one "likes" or "pleases," which would make point II. Something like: "This being understood, do as you please" or ". . . do as you like."

Another occurrence (occasionally erroneously cited as a non Crowley source for the Gnostic Mass elements in Wicca) is the parody of Liber 15 (cap 22: "As to a Veil They Broke") in James Branch Cabell's (1879-1958) Jurgen: [3]

Anaïtis answered: "There is no law in Cocaigne save, Do that which seems good to you."
Then said the naked children: "Perhaps it is the law, (p. 156)

Cabell corresponded with Crowley and was heavily influenced by the French farcical fantasies of which Pausole is indicative and which Cabell's works are conscious stylistic imitations.

P.S. It is also interesting to note that the Ella Wheeler Wilcox who Gardner quotes in The Meaning of Witchcraft, in the context of the ethics of Witchcraft, was one of the founders of modern Rosicrucianism [4] in America, an associate of Spencer Lewis's and one of the first officers of AMORC. Considering GBG's involvement with various Rosicrucian orders (cf. Heselton and Hutton) and the relationship

between AMORC and OTO this is quite
interesting.

------
notes

1. Louÿs, Pierre. Les Aventures Du Roi Pausole.
Paris: Albin Michel, 1948.
2. Louÿs, Pierre. The Adventures of King
Pausole. trans. Charles H. Lumley, illus.
Beresford Egan. New York: William Godwin, 1933.
3. Cabell, James Branch. Jurgen: a Comedy of
Justice. New York: R.M. McBride & Company,
1922, c1919.
(http://docsouth.unc.edu/cabell/menu.html)
4. Palo, Dr. John. "Ella Wheeler Wilcox (1850-
1919): Writer and Mystic Rosicrucian."
Rosicrucian Library.
(http://www.crcsite.org/Wilcox.htm).

And the Second Letter which goes into much more detail:

From: "Jones, David R."
Cc: list@geraldgardner.com
Subject: RE: Good King Pausol?
Date: Thu, 26 Jul 2001

Do what thou wilt

Shall be the whole of the Law.

   King Pausole is sometimes erroneously
attributed to Rabelais, because LeRoy Pausole
is of course using a variant of the Rabelaisian
dictum, from the portal of the Abbey of Thelema
(1), and hence the relationship to Crowley's
first Law (2). From what I have seen of book
and its derivative theatrical forms it
certainly seems heavily influenced by Rabelais
on many levels.

   King Pausol is in fact not legendary per se
but the literary creation from the French novel
by Pierre Louÿs 9(1870-1925): Les Aventures du
roi Pausole : Pausole (souverain paillard et
débonnaire)(1901 and reprinted in 1925 numerous

times since), or the Adventures of King Pausole
(the bawdy and good natured sovereign). An
image of the frontpiece of the 1st edt. can be
found at the Gallica online library [3a] along
with a Table of Contents and a promise of text
[3b]. I have appended the Table of Contents [i]
and my computer aided translation would seem to
indicate to me that Book 1 Chapter 4 is
probably the place to look, but this is just a
guess. The work looks to be Victorian erotica,
as do the other works of Louÿs [3a]. One
reviewer described the book as "Fine, funny,
risqué novel of the king of a strange country,
who has a thousand wives, and believes in
sexual freedom for everyone except his own
daughter Aline. Aline finally runs away with a
"boy" who is really a disguised girl." [5]

Louys, Pierre. The adventures of King
Pausole. London : The Fortune Press, 1919.
Collected works of Pierre Louys. New York :
Liveright, Inc, 1932 (illust. H. G. Spanner).
New York : Shakespeare House, 1951. New York :
Liveright, 1952; [5] as well as at least a
Danish translation Kong Pausole (trans. Svend
Johansen). Though I cannot find it in GBG's
library list the various versions of it (vide
supra et post): French, English, Operetta and
Film make it likely that GBG knew it from one
or more sources.

Louys, Pierre   The book was used as the basis
of an Operetta: Les Aventures du roi Pausole
(1930) by the Swiss composer Arthur Honegger
(1892-1955)[6] and the French librettists
Arthur Willemetz (1887-1964)[7]. GBG could
certainly have seen a performance given the
time frame. A modern recording is available
[8], the operetta is popular enough to rate
modern performances [9]. How much French GBG
knew is not something I have any idea of? It
was common for male Brits to have passable
schoolboy fluency in it, as witnessed decent
translations from that language by his near
contemporaries Crowley, Mathers, Wescott and
Waite. Arthur Honegger was a lesser-known
modern classical composer, associated with
Schoenberg and Stravinsky (both of whom were

heavily influenced by pagan themes). Willemetz
was a famous librettist of the French comedic
theatre and a popular biography by his daughter
is available.

The book was also made into a film directed
by Alexis Granowsky [10] (released 1933)
featuring the Swiss born Austrian actor Emil
Jannings (1884-1950, Oscar for best actor in
The Way of All Flesh, 1927 and The Last Command
1928): released variously under the titles Die
Abenteuer des Königs Pausole (Germany), König
Pausole (Austria), King Pausole (Great Britain)
and The Merry Monarch (USA) [11]. According to
the storyline the plot goes: "Happy king
Pausole reigns peacefully on the kingdom of
Triphème. Each night, to share its layer, it
chooses one of its 366 wives who live all in
waiting of this annual event. The life runs out
calmly until the arrival of an aviator who,
falling under the charm from the girl from
Pausole, hustles the practices of the palace."
[12] Available in video [13]

I am in the process of getting most of this
material via Interlibrary Loan and will keep
you all informed, regarding its relation to the
Rede and the dictum of will as its categorical
imperative.

[1.]

[2.]
Liber 220: I:

[3.]
a.

http://gallica.bnf.fr/scripts/ConsultationTout.
exe?E=0&O=N081090

1906 & 1931
http://www.passiperduti.com/ristersomm.asp?CTS=
843&NDP=37

1925

http://gallica.bnf.fr/metacata.idq?Cirestrictio
n=@_Auteur(LOUYS%20PIERRE)
http://www.loiseaulire.com/Litterature/France/L
ouys.html

1938
http://www.livre-rare-
book.com/Matieres/dd/2373.html
1947
http://myfreesurf.aucland.fr/accdb/viewItem.asp
?IDI=1390101
http://www.loiseaulire.com/Litterature/France/L
ouys.html

b.
http://gallica.bnf.fr/scripts/ConsultationTout.
exe?E=0&O=N080804

[4.]
http://www.france.diplomatie.fr/culture/france/
musique/composit/honegger.html

[5.]
http://www.queerreads.com/page0229.htm

[6.]
http://www.france.diplomatie.fr/culture/france/
musique/composit/honegger.html

[7.]
http://us.imdb.com/Name?Willemetz,+Albert
http://www.multimania.com/musicom/auteurs_auteu
rs_willemetz.html
http://www.intac.com/~rfrone/operas/sfo/operasa
/Aventures_du_Roi_Parusole.htm

[8.]
http://shopping.yahoo.com/shop?d=c&id=171783

[9.]
Video
http://www.alsapresse.com/jdj/98/01/17/ST/page_
1.html
for some details with a rather cute picture of
the cast at:

http://www.alsapresse.com/jdj/98/01/17/ST/photo
_1.html

[10.]
http://us.imdb.com/Title?0272729

[11.
http://homepages.about.com/unofficialoscars/osc
ars/actors/jannings.html

[12.]
http://www.lamediatheque.be/Mediaquest/Recherch
e?ACTION=Details&COLLECTION=C
inema&REFERENCE=VA8549+

[13.]
http://www.lamediatheque.be/EVENEMENTS/EDWIGEFE
UILLERE/EDWIGEFEUILLERE.htm

Appendix

i.
Louÿs (P.) . Les Aventures du roi Pausole :
Pausole (souverain paillard et
débonnaire).

TABLE DES MATIÈRES

LIVRE PREMIER

ii.

~ Appendix C ~
The Old Laws (1961)[1]

These were the Laws of the Craft per Gerald Gardner. There was much controversy as to the legitimacy of these laws since they had apparently been "discovered" by Gardner at a time when such laws would have been convenient to him.

[A] The Law was made and Ardane of old. The law was made for the Wicca, to advise and help in their troubles. The Wicca should give due worship to the Gods and obey their will, which they Ardane, for it was made for the good of the Wicca, As the Wicca's worship is good for the Gods, For the Gods love the Wicca. As a man loveth a woman, by mastering her, so the Wicca should love the Gods, by being mastered by them. And it is necessary that the Circle, which is the Temple of the Gods, should be truly cast and purified, that it may be a fit place for the Gods to enter. And the Wicca should be properly prepared and purified, to enter into the presence of the Gods. With love and worship in their hearts they shall raise power from their bodies to give power to the Gods, as has been taught us of old, For in this way only may man have communion with the Gods, for the Gods cannot help man without the help of men.

---

[1] Publicly available at sacred-texts.com, which is an invaluable service worth supporting!

[B] And the High Priestess shall rule her Coven as representative of the Goddess, and the High Priest shall support her as the representative of the God, And the High Priestess shall choose whom she will, if he have sufficient rank, to be her High Priest), For the God himself, kissed her feet in the fivefold salute, laying his power at the feet of the Goddess, because of her youth and beauty, her sweetness and kindness, her wisdom and Justice, her humility and generosity. So he resigned his lordship to her. But the Priestess should ever mind that all power comes from him. It is only lent when it is used wisely and justly. And the greatest virtue of a High Priestess is that she recognizes that youth is necessary to the representative of the Goddess, so that she will retire gracefully in favour of a younger woman, Should the Coven so decide in Council, For the true High Priestess realizes that gracefully surrendering pride of place is one of the greatest of virtues, and t hat thereby she will return to that pride of place in another life, with greater power and beauty.

[C] In the days when Witchdom extended far, we were free and worshipped in All their Greatest Temples, but in these unhappy times we must hold our sacred mysteries in secret. So it be Ardane, that none but the Wicca may see our mysteries, for our enemies are many, And torture looseth the tongues of many. It be Ardane that each Coven shall not know where the next Coven bide, or who its members are, save the Priest and Priestess, That there shall be no communication between them, save by the Messenger of the Gods, or the Summoner. Only if it be safe, may the Covens meet, in some safe place, for the great festivals. And while there, none shall say whence they come, or give their true names, to the end that, if any are tortured, in their agony, they can not tell if they know not. So it be Ardane that no one may tell any not of the Craft who be of the Wicca, nor give any names, or where they bide, or in any way tell anything which can betray any to our foes, nor may they tell where the Covenstead be, or where is the Covendom, or where be the meeting s or that there have been meetings. And if any break these laws, even under torture, The Curse of the Goddess shall be upon them, so they never reborn on earth, And may they remain where they belong, in the Hell of the Christians.

[D] Let each High Priestess govern her Coven with Justice and love, with the help of the advice of the elders, always heeding the advice of the Messenger of the Gods, if he cometh. She will heed all complaints of brothers, and strive to settle all differences among them, but it must be recognized that there be people who will ever strive to force others to do as they will. They are not necessarily evil, and they often do have good ideas, and such ideas should be talked over in council. And if they will not agree with their brothers, or if they say, "I will not work under this High Priestess," it hath always been the old law to be convenient for the brethren, and to void disputes, any of the Third may claim to found a new Coven because they live over a league from the Covenstead, or are about to do so. Anyone living within the Covendom wishing to form a new Coven, to avoid strife, shall tell the Elders of his intention and on the instant void his dwelling and remove to the new Covendom. Members of the old Coven may join the New one when it be formed, but if they do, must utterly void the old Coven. The Elders of the New and the Old Covens should meet in peace and brotherly love, to decide the new boundaries. Those of the Craft who dwell outside both Covendoms may join either indifferent, but not both, though all may, if the Elders agree, meet for the Great Festivals, if it be truly in peace and brotherly love. But splitting the coven oft means strife, so for this reason these laws were made of old, And may the curse of the Goddess be on any who disregard them. So be it ardane.

[E] If you would Keep a book let it be in your own hand of write. Let brothers and sisters copy what they will, but never let the book out of your hands, and never keep the writings of another, for if it be found in their hand of write, they well may be taken and enjoined. Each should guard his own writings and destroy it whenever danger threatens. Learn as much as you may by heart, and when danger is past, rewrite your book an it be safe. For this reason, if any die, destroy their book if they have not been able to, for an it be found, 'tis clear proof against them, And our oppressors well know, "Ye may not be a witch alone" So all their kin and friends be in danger of torture. So ever destroy anything not necessary. If your book be found on you. 'tis clear proof against you alone. You may be enjoined. Keep all thoughts of the Craft from your mind. Say you had bad dreams; a devil caused you to write it without your knowledge. Think to yourself, "I know nothing. I remember nothing. I have forgotten everything." Drive this into your mind. If the torture be too great to bear, say, "I will confess. I cannot bear this torture. What do you want me to say? Tell me and I will say it." If they try to make you speak of the brotherhood, Do NOT, but if they try to make you speak of impossibilities, such as flying through the air, consorting with the Christian Devil, or sacrificing children, or eating men's flesh, to obtain relief from torture, say, "I had an evil dream. I was not myself. I was crazed." Not all Magistrates are bad. If there be an excuse they may show mercy. If you have confessed aught, deny it afterwards; say you babbled under torture, you knew not what you did or said. If you are condemned, fear not. The Brotherhood is powerful. They may help you to escape, if you stand steadfast, but if you betray aught, there is no hope for you, in this life, or in that which is to come. Be sure, if steadfast you go to the pyre, Dwale will reach you. You will feel naught. You go but to o Death and what lies beyond, the ecstasy of the Goddess.

[F] 'Tis probable that before you are enjoined, Dwale will reach you. Always remember that Christians fear much that any die under torture. At the first sign of swoon, they cause it to be stopped, and blame the tormenters. For that reason, the tormenters themselves are apt to feign to torment, but do not, so it is best not to die at first. If Dwale reaches you, 'tis a sign that you have a friend somewhere. You may be helped to escape, so despair not. If the worst comes, and you go to the pyre, wait till the flames and smoke spring up, bend your head over, and breath in with long breaths. You choke and die swiftly, and wake in the arms of the Goddess.

[G] To void discovery, let the working tools be as ordinary things that any may have in their houses. Let the Pentacles be of wax, so they may be broken at once. Have no sword unless your rank allows you one. Have no names or signs on anything. Write the names and signs on them in ink before consecrating them and wash it off immediately after. Do not Bigrave them, lest they cause discovery. Let the colour of the hilts tell which is which.

[H] Ever remember, ye are the Hidden Children of the Gods. So never do anything to disgrace them. Never boast, Never threaten, Never say you would wish ill to anyone. If you or any not in the Circle speak of the Craft, say, "Speak not to me of such. It frightens me. 'Tis evil luck to speak of it." For this reason: the Christians have spies everywhere. These speak as if they were well affected, as if they would come to Meetings, saying, "My mother used to go to worship the Old Ones. I would that I could go myself." To these ever deny all knowledge. But to others ever say, "'Tis foolish men talk of witches flying through the air; to do so they must be light as thistledown," and "Men say that witches all be bleared-eyed old crones, so what pleasure can there be in witch meetings such as folk talk on?" Say, "Many wise men now say there be no such creatures." Ever make it a jest, and in some future time, perhaps the persecution will die, and we may worship safely again. Let us all pray for that happy day.

[I] May the blessings of the Goddess and the God be on all who keep these laws which are Ardane.

[J] If the Craft hath any Appanage, let all brothers guard it, and help to keep it clear and good for the Craft, and let all justly guard all monies of the Craft. But if some brothers truly wrought it, 'tis right that they have their pay, an it be just, an this be not taking money for the use of the Art, but for good and honest work. And even the Christians say, "A labourer is worthy of his hire." But if any brothers willingly for the good of the craft without pay, 'tis but to their greater honour. So it be Ardane.

[K] If there be any disputes or quarrels among the brethren, the High Priestess shall straight convene the Elders and enquire into the matter, and they shall hear both sides, first alone, then together, and they shall decide justly, not favouring the one side or the other, ever recognizing that there be people who can never agree to work under others, but at the same time there be some people who cannot rule justly. To those who ever must be chief, there is one answer, "Void the Coven and seek an other, or make a Coven of your own, taking with you those who will to go." To those who cannot rule justly, the answer be, "Those who cannot bear your rule will leave you," for none may come to meetings with those with whom they are at variance; so, an either cannot agree, get hence, for the Craft must ever survive. So it be Ardane.

[L] In the olden days when we had power, we could use our Arts against any who ill-treated any of the Brotherhood, but in these evil times, we may not do so, for our enemies have devised a burning pit of everlasting fire, into which they say their God casteth all the people who worship him, except it be the very few who are released by their priests' spells and Masses, and this be chiefly by giving money and rich gifts to receive his favour, for their Alther Greatest God [Greatest God of all] is ever in need of Money. But as our Gods need our aid to make fertility for men and crops, So the God of the Christians is ever in need of man's help to search out and destroy us. Their priests tell them that any who get our help or our cures are damned to the Hell forever, so men be mad for the terror of it. But they make men believe that they may scape this hell if they give victims to the tormenters. So for this reason all be forever spying, thinking, "An I can but catch one of the Wicca I will scape this fiery pit." But we have our hidels, and men searching long and not finding say, "there be none, or if they be, they be in a far country." But when one of our oppressors die, or even be sick, ever is the cry, "This be Witches Malice," and the hunt is up again. And though they slay ten of their people to one of ours, still they care not; they have many thousands, while we are few indeed. So it is Ardane that none shall use the Art in any way to do ill to any, howevermuch they have injured us. And for long we have obeyed this law, "Harm none" and nowtimes many believe we exist not. So it be Ardane that this law shall still continue to help us in our plight. No one, however great an injury or injustice they receive, may use the Art in any to do ill or harm any. But they may, after great consultations with all, use the Art to prevent or restrain Christians from harming us and others, but only to let or constrain them and never to punish, to this end. Men say, "Such an one is a mighty searcher out and persecutor of Old Women whom he deemeth to be Witches, and none hath done him Skith [harm], so this be proof they cannot, or more truly, that there be none," For all know full well that so many folk have died because someone had a grudge against them, or were persecuted because they had money or goods to seize, or because they had none to bribe the searchers. And many have died because they were scolding old women, so much so that men now say that only old women are witches, and this be to our advantage, and turns suspicion away from us. In England 'tis now many a year since a witch hath died the death, but any misuse of the power might raise the Persecution again; so never break this law, however much you are tempted, and never consent to its being broken. If you know it is being broken in the least, you must work strongly against it, and any High Priestess or High Priest who consents to it must be immediately deposed, for 'tis the blood of the Brethren they endanger. Do good, an it be safe, and only if it be safe, for any talk may endanger us.

[M] And strictly keep to the Old Law, never accept money for the use of the art. It is Christian priests and sorcerers who accept money for the use of their Arts, and they sell Dwale and evil love spells and pardons to let men scape from their sins. Be not as these. Be not as these. If you accept not money, you will be free of temptation to use the Art for evil causes.

[N] You may use the Art for your own advantage, or for the advantage of the Craft, only if you be sure you harm none. But ever let the Coven debate the matter at length. Only if all are satisfied that none may be harmed may the Art be used. If it is not possible to achieve your ends one way without harming any, perchance the aim may be achieved by acting in a different way, so as to harm none. May the Curse of the Goddess be on any who breach this law. So it be Ardane.

[O] 'Tis adjudged lawful an anyone need a house or land, an none will sell, to incline the owner's mind to be willing to sell, provided it harmeth him not in any way, and that the full worth is paid, without haggling. Never bargain or cheapen anything which you buy by the Art. So it be Ardane.

[P] It is the Old Law and the most important of all Laws that no one may do or say anything which will endanger any of the Craft, or bring them in contact with the law of the land, or the Law of the Church or any of our persecutors. In any disputes between the brethren, no one may invoke any laws but those of the Craft, or any Tribunal but that of the Priestess and the Priest and the Elders. And may the Curse of the Goddess be on any who so do. So it be Ardane.

[Q] It is not forbidden to say as Christians do, "There be Witchcraft in the Land," because our oppressors of old made it Heresy not to believe in Witchcraft, and so a crime to deny it, which thereby put you under suspicion. But ever say "I know not of it here, perchance they may be, but afar off. I know not where." But ever speak so you cause others to doubt they be as they are. Always speak of them as old crones, consorting with the Devil and riding through the air. But ever say, "But how may men ride through the air an they be not as light as thistledown?" But the curse of the Goddess be on any who cast any suspicion on any of the Brotherhood, or speaks of any real meeting place, or where any bide. So it be Ardane.

[R] Let the Craft keep books with the names of all Herbs which are good for man, and all cures, that all may learn. But keep another book with all the Banes [poisons] and Apies. and let only the elders and trustworthy people have this knowledge. So it be Ardane.

[S] And may the Blessings of the Gods be on all who keep these Laws and the Curses of both God and Goddess be on all who break them So it be Ardane.

[The following two sections were added after 1960.]

[T] Remember the Art is the secret of the Gods and may only be used in earnest and never for show or vainglory. Magicians and Christians may taunt us, saying, "You have no power. Do magic before our eyes. Then only will we believe," seeking to cause us to betray our Art before them. Heed them not, for the Art is holy, and may only be used in need. And the curse of the Gods be on any who break this law.

[U] It ever be the way with women, and with men also, that they ever seek new love, nor should we reprove them for this, but it may be found to disadvantage the Craft, as so many a time it has happened that a High Priest or High Priestess, impelled by love, hath departed with their love; that is, they have left the coven. Now, if a High Priestess wishes to resign, she may do so in full Coven, and this resignation is valid. But if they should run off without resigning, who may know if they may not return w within a few months? So the law is, if a High Priestess leaves her coven, but returns within the space of a year and a day, then she shall be taken back, and all shall be as before. Meanwhile, if she has a deputy, that deputy shall act as High Priestess for as long as the High Priestess is away. If she returns not at the end of a year and a day, then shall the coven elect a new High Priestess. Unless there be a good reason to the contrary. The person who has done the work should reap the benefit of the reward, Maiden and deputy of the High Priestess.

About the Author

John J. Coughlin has been a practitioner of the Occult Arts since the mid-1980's. In that time he has worked with several groups, although he primarily prefers to walk a solitary, eclectic path. His pivotal work *Out of the Shadows* has lead some to consider him the father of Dark Paganism, given he was the first author to publically explore that concept.

Currently, John is the founder and book binder of Waning Moon Publications and Editor/Webmaster of the NYC Pagan Resource Guide. He has also created many other web-based projects for Pagans, Goths, and other specialized groups which can be found on waningmoon.com.

A relatively reclusive author in occult circles, John's other public books include *Out of the Shadows: An Exploration of Dark Paganism and Magick, Liber Yog-Sothoth,* and *A Cthulhian Grimoire of Dream Work.* His written work extends onto the Internet in his ongoing and heavily-researched study of the history and evolution of Wiccan ethics.

Index